WORLD WAR 2 HISTORY FOR KIDS

• • • • • • • • • •

WORLD WAR 2 HISTORY FOR KIDS

© Copyright 2023 - All rights reserved.

Published 2023 by History Brought Alive

The content contained within this book may not be reproduced, duplicated, or transmitted without direct written permission from the author or the publisher.

Under no circumstances will any blame or legal responsibility be held against the publisher, or author, for any damages, reparation, or monetary loss due to the information contained within this book, either directly or indirectly.

LEGAL NOTICE:

This book is copyright protected. It is only for personal use. You cannot amend, distribute, sell, use, quote, or paraphrase any part, or the content within this book, without the consent of the author or publisher.

DISCLAIMER NOTICE:

Please note the information contained within this document is for educational and entertainment purposes only. All effort has been executed to present accurate, up-to-date, reliable, complete information. No warranties of any kind are declared or implied. Readers acknowledge that the author is not engaged in the rendering of legal, financial, medical, or professional advice. The content within this book has been derived from various sources. Please consult a licensed professional before attempting any techniques outlined in this book.

By reading this document, the reader agrees that under no circumstances is the author responsible for any losses, direct or indirect, that are incurred as a result of the use of the information contained within this document, including, but not limited to, errors, omissions, or inaccuracies.

FREE BONUS FROM HBA: EBOOK BUNDLE

Greetings!

First, thank you for reading our books.

Now, we invite you to join our VIP list. As a welcome gift we offer the History & Mythology eBook Bundle below for free. Plus, you can be the first to receive new books and exclusives! Remember it's 100% free to join.

Simply click the link below to join.

https://www.subscribepage.com/hba

Keep up to date with us on:
YouTube: History Brought Alive
Facebook: History Brought Alive
www.historybroughtalive.com

CONTENTS

INTRODUCTION 1

A QUICK PEEK INTO LIFE BACK THEN 5
WHY DO WE NEED TO EVEN LEARN ABOUT WARS? 7
WHAT TO EXPECT FROM THIS BOOK 10

CHAPTER 1: WHEN EACH THOUGHT THEY WERE RIGHT 15

THE AXIS VERSUS THE ALLIES 19
THE WORLD SEES WAR — FOR THE SECOND TIME 23
MORE AND MORE NATIONS GET SUCKED INTO THE FIGHT 25
ATTACKS, DEFENSES, AND MORE ATTACKS! 27

CHAPTER 2: THE POT IS BOILING AND THE ARENA IS HEATING UP 30

ITALY 32
JAPAN 34
GERMANY 36
BATTLELINES ARE DRAWN AT A FEVERISH PACE 39
A SERIES OF CONQUESTS GAIN PACE 41
ITALY BEGINS TO HIT ROADBLOCKS 42
ACTION IN ASIA 44

CHAPTER 3: GETTING MILLIONS OF PEOPLE TO THINK AS THEY DESIRED 48

WHEN EVERYONE THINKS THE SAME WAY - A GOOD THING OR BAD? 50
THE JAPANESE STORY 54
BUT WHY DID JAPAN ATTACK AMERICA? 58
THE AMERICAN STORY 59

CHAPTER 4: LIFE ON THE HOMEFRONT 64

RATIONING AND SHORTAGES 67
PROPAGANDA AND CENSORSHIP 70
INTERNMENT OF JAPANESE-AMERICANS 73

CHAPTER 5: TURNING POINTS OF THE WAR 79

- Invasion of Poland, but Why? 81
- Battle of Britain 84
- Invasion of the Soviet Union and the Battle of Stalingrad 85
- D-Day Invasion 88
- Attack on Pearl Harbor, December 7th, 1941 90

CHAPTER 6: THE HOLOCAUST 94

- What Caused The Hatred? 96
- What Makes Normal People Do Cruel Acts? 99
- What Went on in the Extermination Camps 102

CHAPTER 7: END OF WAR 108

- The Battle of Berlin and the V-E Day 110
- Dropping The Atomic Bomb and the V-J Day 112
- We Need a Tolerant World to Thrive and Dream 115
- The United Nations Organization 119

CHAPTER 8: BUT WHAT ABOUT ME, MY DREAMS, DON'T THEY MATTER? 122

- Ordinary People When Their Country Went To War 123
- How Does It Feel to Migrate and Resettle? 127
- In the Diary of Anne Frank 129
- When Ordinary People Did Extraordinary Things 132
- A Story Untold—of the Japanese Americans 136

CHAPTER 9: LIFESTYLE, INVENTIONS, AND NEW IDEAS 140

- Here We Come, the Ghost Army 143
- Learning to Live in Different Ways 144
- The Family Looks Different 148
- Schools During Wars 150
- Overcoming Despair Through Sports 152

CHAPTER 10: LIFESTYLE, INVENTIONS, AND NEW IDEAS 156

    YUMI'S BROTHER, JAPAN 1942 157
    CLAUS'S FRIEND GOES MISSING, GERMANY 1940 159
    HAUNTING MEMORIES TO LIVE WITH, VIETNAM 1943 .161
    THE DAY IT RAINED PARACHUTES, NETHERLANDS 1944 163
    SEA, AN ESCAPE? DENMARK 1943.............................. 165

CONCLUSION 169

    BYSTANDER OR UPSTANDER: WHAT DO YOU SAY? 175

REFERENCES 181

INTRODUCTION

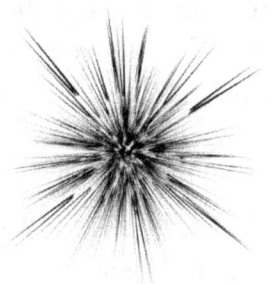

History Brought Alive

"Hey, Ben!" I heard the chirpy voice of my sister behind me. I had just gotten back home after serving in the war zone for fourteen months, and it felt so good to be back with my family. "Jenny told me that her school principal mentioned how the students should be proud of the brave soldiers of our country. Now she thinks you are Superman and wants to know everything about your work." she smiled. I would love to talk to my ten-year-old niece about my days as a trooper. It has taken me to so many places far from home. I got to see for myself how people live and think in very unique ways. I learned to understand their feelings and respect them even though we are quite different. It is a lot of hard work and is challenging but then so satisfying. I can't wait to tell her how fortunate we are to be living in a peaceful country where we can follow our dreams.

(National World War 2 Memorial)

Our parents are survivors of the Second World War, and my sister and I have grown up listening to countless stories of how it was to live as little kids in those terrible days. Dad remembers how his favorite cousin sacrificed his life for his country. Mamma tells us how her family had to go hungry at times because the food was not available in the market. A lot of their memories were filled with sadness and fear, but also had many stories of kindness, hope, bravery, and sacrifice. They would tell me how their days in the countryside were spent in bunkers, going to bed every night unsure if they would wake up safe the next day, or seeing their parents go out and wondering if they would return safely. I am all grown up, but those stories still make me feel heavy with emotions.

There was also an interesting twist in the tale. My dad would often talk of how during those traumatizing days, a rather unexpected wave of goodness and hope would overtake the mood in the bunkers. It was almost like suddenly feeling great value for life because death was such a strong possibility. People would be extremely kind, caring, and compassionate to each other. He said it is rather amusing to now think of how there would be no petty fights, jealousy, or bullying amongst the people in the neighborhood, that were otherwise found during normal times. Does that mean we need wars to bring out the best in us? I hope not. My parents are old and truly hope that their future generations never get to see a war. Who wouldn't agree, right? But would you agree with me that we need to know what exactly happened, the reason for the war, and what came out of it? We need those answers to understand how fights can be resolved in a much better way.

As an adult, I still have unanswered questions. What started such a big fight that it took so many years and millions of people dying, and many more suffering to find an answer finally? How did one guy come to believe that by harming another group of people he was serving his people; and how did he even manage to persuade others to act per his wishes? We are taught to be kind and to share, and we know for sure that being mean does not bring us any reward. But then, why did people behave badly with others? We need to know.

A Quick Peek Into Life Back Then

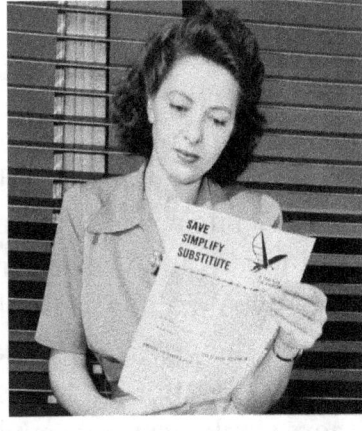

When we talk about wars of the past I think we also need to know how people lived during those times. We will then maybe understand why the wars began in the first place. Even a hundred years back, people lived a very different life compared to what we are used to. We live in a world where we usually don't have to worry about getting food to eat, a home to stay, or medicines when we are sick. We don't think twice about boarding a bus to school, a plane to travel, or saving up for a cruise during the summer holidays. Of course, we need to work hard to earn each one of these, but then they are available to choose from. Do you remember ever walking into the supermarket with money, and them telling you, "Sorry, but the bread will not be available until next Wednesday, we'll have to be patient"? Today, progress in scientific learning and technology is allowing for food, medicines, security, and everything we wish to have, to be available around us. We have choices, but this was not the case then.

Up until about two hundred years back, getting food to eat and a place to live was not as easy and things were quite uncertain when compared to our times. If food was not available it meant the people would suffer, not just some people, but a whole community could perish. And food could vanish for several reasons—the crops would fail because there would be no rain during the year, and diseases and pests would cause vegetation and livestock to die. At times there would be more people than there was food because the population would have increased. To make sure everyone had enough to eat and survive, they would have to make more land available to them. This would mean using force to get land from other communities and in the struggle, the stronger people would destroy the weaker. Survival of the fittest is the law of nature, but it took the form of war among human beings. We could surely use our imagination to make better choices so that we all live well without hurting one another.

Wars for survival have been part of human civilization for thousands of years. But it did not stop there. Wars continued and became nastier even after the security of food and safety was taken care of. We might need to put on our thinking caps at this point. The world has progressed because we have learned from past mistakes. Technology is allowing us to make sure everyone gets a chance to improve their lives. When talking about conflict, it is not enough to look at war only as adults see it. It can feel strange to think of a war situation where our lives could turn upside down. The feelings, fears, and answers that children have are sometimes lost to the grown-ups. It is so important that everyone starts listening to children as well.

Why Do We Need To Even Learn About Wars?

The other day my seven-year-old nephew returned home in the afternoon looking puzzled. He said his class was collecting toys to donate to children who had lost their belongings in a flood. The trouble was that he could not understand why he had to part with his toy when he did not know any of the people who were affected. The flood had happened thousands of miles away. Can I ask you to think about another situation? Imagine you find out that a new family has moved into your apartment, and that they are from a different country—they look different, speak a strange language, and have mannerisms you are not used to—would it trigger discomfort? Think of your instinctive reactions and make a note of your responses. They behave strangely. I should stay away from them; versus I am curious to know them better. Perhaps you will take the second option, but then your friends tease you for that and so you take the first option unwillingly, to avoid being spotlighted.

It is easy to dislike someone because they look different. I think the brain feels unsafe and threatened. We don't understand their problems because we are so busy hating them. But we need to be able to stop our train of thought and look at the same thing differently. It might surprise us that a single decision to relook at the situation will give us a completely different story. If these situations are putting you in a fix, you are not alone. Like you, I wonder why conflict comes about in the first place. There is confusion about how to act in a certain situation. We face dilemmas every other day. It could be when you feel that your older brother is behaving in unfair ways and bullying you into giving up your favorite things, or when you feel tempted to yank that chocolate from the baby's hands when nobody's looking.

I'm sure we all want to know why we feel the way we do. We want to be able to sort out things in a way that does not harm anyone. This is where knowing history comes in handy. We can learn from mistakes people have already committed. We learn to put ourselves in the place of people who suffer, and that would make parting with his toys easier for my nephew. It allows us to be understanding of others' feelings even if we don't know them or we strongly disagree with them. Challenge your notions about things, and you will find yourself growing as a person. When we learn from the mistakes of the past, we will not repeat those blunders, and this gives us a better chance of doing what is right.

Believe me, even grown-ups don't like to think of war, because even the winning side suffers from all the disturbances that come along. You would agree that anybody would want to have another chance at proving their point in a much better way. But then things are not always black or white. The reasons why people do what they do can be complex and it would take us time to understand the full context. We need to keep our minds open and be patient in many situations.

We have another problem. Wars are not exactly things of the past. We are also the first

generation of human beings to be watching war happen live on television, sitting in our living rooms. That makes it all the more difficult for us because it feels like war is at our doorstep and we can do nothing about it. We have so many questions, and so many feelings, but no answers. Let us take time to talk, ask questions, or maybe even write down our thoughts, they all help.

What To Expect From This Book

Great wars were fought in the past and revisiting them is a helpful way of knowing more about ourselves, about human behavior. Stories of the war scare us and fascinate us at the same time. But understanding whatever happened a while back helps us know the consequences of people's actions. And from them, we can learn our lessons and become better people. Through the stories about why a war started and how it progressed, we will be in a position to form opinions on how people think and react to situations. We learn that our feelings about people or a situation can sometimes work against us. When we can think well we make good choices. So I think learning history will help us make sensible decisions in our own life. We become better at life skills which, I am sure, will make us happier and more compassionate. There is another bonus to reading about events in the world. When you know a lot of facts, it will make you an informed person and more popular. After all, who does not like to have a smart friend—emotionally and intellectually?

I get that the stories will sometimes make us feel bad about what happened. But not to worry, because they also demonstrate how bravery, kindness, and a positive attitude even in the face of severe challenges can provide hope and inspiration. Doesn't it feel good to know that things can turn bright even when they seem to be all glum, and that an optimistic mind always comes up with solutions? If we can turn our kindness into action, things would be so much better.

Many years have passed since the two world wars, and all of us have the chance to think about what happened. It took these wars to teach us that fighting only brings destruction and even more hard feelings. It has also inspired many people to write stories and poems, make films and art, and come up with new ideas for solving problems. It helps us take a peek into the complex human mind. It is forcing all of us to look at how we want to deal with problems in the future, and that is a good thing. The governments of the modern world have put together ideas so that we can control situations by talking to each other and not by attacking the opposite side. We all need to work hard to protect the peace in society. For that, remembering the wars is very important. If we take peace for granted and forget about the consequences of violence, are we not in danger of slipping back into the same mistakes made in the past?

In this book, we will get to read about many thrilling events and fascinating stories of heroes, ordinary men, women, and children who demonstrated that being kind, brave, and selfless can help us come out of bad situations. War is in many ways similar to situations we face in our daily lives. I'm sure a teasing remark by a friend or witnessing an argument at home can also trigger a war in your mind. There is a risk that things may become tense, but there is also a chance that you will act thoughtfully to resolve it. You see, if the challenge had not come about in the first place, nobody would have known you were such a mature and sensible person.

Oh yes, and there is something else in store. Consider this. When we get into danger, apart from trying to get away from it, what else do we do? We use our imagination and creativity to solve problems that are thrown at us. Now, is that not a beautiful thing to be able to do? There were a lot of discoveries and inventions that were made by the scientific community and ordinary people to help with the war. Some of them were brilliant enough to stay forever and continue to change lives to this day. Yup! We will be talking about these amazing developments as we progress.

CHAPTER 1
WHEN EACH THOUGHT THEY WERE RIGHT

• • • • • • • • •

It was about a hundred years ago when it all began. World War II was the second conflict that qualified as a "world" war because of the number of countries that were affected. It sparked out in the year 1939 and blazed on for the next six years. Six years of grave difficulties, for the people, for the governments, for the countries that were not even directly part of the war! But how did it all begin, and what came out of it? We need to retrace time a bit more to get the back story: to 1914. That was when the First World War had erupted. But what happened during the first one? And are the two connected? We will soon find out.

The countries in the European continent were great powers at that time. They were using their inventions, like steam engines, electricity, and guns, to colonize many other nations around the world and introduce industrialization to human society. What is colonization? It is about a group going to another country, taking control of it, and making the people of that nation behave as per their wishes. What is industrialization? To put it simply, it is the ability to use natural resources, like land, water, forests, and minerals, to manufacture things in large quantities. That meant anybody who had access to large masses of land could control the production of food, clothing, machines, weapons, or anything else, and become powerful in the process.

When countries become powerful, the tension between them also grows, because then each worries that the other country will overpower them. You know the reasons, the more land under one country's control, the richer and more powerful that country gets. Normally it starts peacefully with pacts and agreements being signed. They would agree to not get into each other's way. But along the way, the gentlemanly promises would get broken and conflicts would begin. Similar stories are everywhere! It gets complicated when business interests tempt people to indulge in unfair behavior. Small incidents add up and eventually blow up.

During those times, countries were also run differently. We are now used to having voting rights as citizens, and our opinions matter in how a country works. But it was not the case back then. There were either kings or dictators. This meant that a few powerful people would make decisions on behalf of millions of people. When a country went to war, the people were expected to participate and defend their nation.

We had a situation where each country was generally suspicious of the others. In July 1914, Austria-Hungary declared war on Serbia when the crown prince was assassinated by a Serbian young man. Russia immediately took Serbia's side. What followed was many other countries getting involved by taking sides with their friends or where they saw some benefit. I am sure you can relate to this. Two acquaintances in a neighborhood get into a tussle and in no time

we have people either taking sides or intervening to stop the fight, depending on who they think is right. Yes, sometimes not participating and staying neutral is also an option.

The Axis Versus the Allies

Anyway, over the next few months, the war cascaded into a major one with essentially two teams the Allied Powers and the Central Axis Powers. What started with two countries eventually became nineteen countries from Europe and beyond involved in a four-year-long war. This gives me a feeling that nations then saw fighting as a practical way to solve problems. We have learned bitter lessons, and so today, thankfully, our governments are ready to talk it out and negotiate rather than take up arms. Phew! About 14 million people died and three times the number of people were adversely affected by hunger, relocation, and disease. With the destruction, and exhaustion having forced everyone to rethink strategies, the war finally ended when peace treaties were drawn to bring things to a compromise. The Central Axis Powers headed by Germany faced defeat and had to accept the demands of the Allied Powers. They signed the Treaty of Versailles [say: ver-SAHY] and it meant the defeated nations would pay a heavy price. The conditions included not being allowed to build an army and paying heavy fines that made their people poor for years to come. The war had ended but instability followed.

Now, this does not look like good news. If one party signs a deal to stop the war and goes away feeling completely disgraced and subdued, would that not leave the possibility of them taking revenge? I mean, it's a fair question, right? It seems some people had this feeling back then, too, and had feared another war in the future. It had been twenty-odd years since the First World War ended and old memories appeared to be fading.

(International delegates during the signing of the Peace Terms ending World War I)

Unfortunately, that was just wishful thinking and the worst fears came true. The war came back, this time only deadlier. Germany was struggling with lost pride and life was tough. An Austrian-born German soldier who was part of the first war could not forget the bitterness and swore to take revenge. His conviction and ability to sway people's minds through his passionate speeches gradually made him more and more powerful. His ideas influenced the minds of people so strongly that they saw purpose in their own lives by following him. Adolf Hitler's influence was rising and about to change the destiny of the world.

He sounds like a hero, right? But there is a

problem here. Humankind finds it difficult to forgive him and considers him to be a symbol of cruelty. His answers to his people's problems were rooted in destroying other people, those who he thought did not deserve to live. Was he a man who would go to any lengths to do what he thought was right? Was he a person who took advantage of the difficulties of the German people to get uncontrolled power? We might as well pause to give it some thought.

We hear of war and see things on television that make us scared. While we are always told to be kind and understanding, we wonder how wars are even allowed to happen. We know by now that conflicts also arise in our minds, and it is a natural thing to happen. The choice lies in what needs to be done about them. Let us look at some of the choices. If someone comes to harm you, or you are convinced they would harm you in the future, you may end up hurting them in self-defense and tell yourself that it was the only choice. In another situation, if I am very strong, I could be tempted to use my power to grab something from another person to feel secure. Turns out, these are the same reasons for which individuals and countries justify wars.

The World Sees War —for the Second Time

Adolf Hitler set about his agenda of rearming Germany, despite what was agreed upon to keep the peace in Europe. He was not alone in the quest for power. There were other countries, like Italy, led by a powerful dictator Mussolini, and Japan, wanting to establish supremacy by taking over neighboring nations starting with China. Hitler was on the watch for partners with similar interests as his. Germany signed strategic treaties with Italy and Japan for assurance of support. In 1939, Hitler thought the time was ripe to get on the offensive. He ordered the German army to march into Poland, their neighboring country. This led Great Britain and France to declare war on Germany because they realized it was only a matter of time before Germany would attack them. In the months and years that followed, two teams similar to the First World War, with reconfigurations, were born—the Axis and the Allies. The main leaders of the Axis were Germany, Japan, and Italy. The dominant leaders of the Allies were Russia, America, Britain, France, and China. The world now had the militaries of different nations grouping themselves into two opposing teams.

A fight also gets bigger if many other things are going wrong at the same time. You would agree that a lighted match stick has a better chance of starting a fire if it fell on dry grass than if it fell on green grass. Likewise, we must also look at the other contributing factors to understand how smaller attacks spiraled into ones that involved dozens of countries. In the meantime, tensions were brewing in many regions across Europe and Asia with powerful nations waiting to attack wherever they could. For instance, China was struggling under the grip of cruel attacks by Japan, leading some historians to say that the trigger to the Second World War could be attributed to it as well. Another cause was the nature of leadership in those years. We had many countries being ruled by dictators. This meant that the ordinary people of the country did not have the option of disagreeing with what the government was doing. The term used to describe governing such a society in this way is fascism [say: FA- SHI-zuhm].

More and More Nations Get Sucked into the Fight

If only the tensions were contained to the nations that were directly involved, but too bad, that is only wishful thinking. The nations that began the war were powerful ones that either already had a bunch of other colonized countries under them, or could capture more. Eventually, more than 70 nations got forcefully involved, both directly and otherwise. Japan, for instance, went on a conquering spree of other nations in Asia so that they would have enough supplies to fight the United States. Can you think of what would be needed to fight a war? Yes, to fight big wars one would need millions of people, tons of food to reach them, and raw materials for making weapons, ships, tanks, and aircraft. Then there would be railway lines and bridges needed to transport people and goods from far-off places. Medical facilities and doctors would be needed. Scientists would be asked to work hard to invent machines to destroy the enemies, and technology to effectively communicate with the soldiers. Factories would be set up to make uniforms and shoes for soldiers, and countless other related needs. The only way to manage these needs was to compel neighbors to part with their resources. Unfair, but that is, sadly, how it worked. Nobody was spared.

I got to visit a place called Kanchanaburi in faraway Thailand recently. It is a place situated  thousands of miles away from Europe and even Japan. But it was a place that also saw the tragedies of the Second World War. During the war, Japan invaded Thailand, much like many other nations, and took its people as prisoners. Ordinary men who worked peacefully on the farms or went about doing their jobs were forced to work on constructing railway lines for the benefit of Japan. They worked under horrible conditions. They would be given simple tools like hammers, picks, and shovels, to cut massive chunks of rocks to allow railway lines to be laid through the mountains. They had to work for hours in bad weather and without food because Japan needed things to reach them fast to fight the war somewhere else. Working under such conditions meant sure death for a lot of people and the project earned the name Death Railway. We walked through a pass called the

Hellfire Pass, listening to the audio tour provided to visitors by the War Memorial Museum. Listening to the accounts of the horrible things and looking at the remnants of the railway lines gave us goosebumps, and made me promise myself not to take peaceful times for granted.

Attacks, Defenses, and More Attacks!

To understand how the war progressed let us lay out a timeline to figure out who attacked whom and why.

1939: On September 1st Germany attacks Poland; On September 3rd the United Kingdom and France declare war against Germany

1940: Germany takes control of France and many other regions in Europe

1941: Germany invades the Soviet Union; Japan attacks American and British territories leading them to declare war on Japan

1942: The Axis begins to see defeat; Germany and Italy are pushed back by the Soviet Union

1943: The Axis powers continue to suffer a series of setbacks forcing them to start retreating

1944: The Allies are gaining power in more and more territories; Japan suffers heavy losses

1945: Germany surrenders with the Allies invading; Hitler commits suicide; The United States drops atomic bombs on Japan when it refuses to surrender; The United Nations organization is born

With fighting happening in so many places at the same time, following it in a neat pattern would be impossible, and so we are going to look at all the important events separately and in chunks. This will also help you understand the big picture, like putting together bits and pieces of a big jigsaw puzzle to get to the full image.

(Berlin protest against the Treaty of Versailles. 1919.)

CHAPTER 2
THE POT IS BOILING AND THE ARENA IS HEATING UP

• • • ● • ● • • •

Think of what happens when two classmates get into an argument over a missing Pokémon card. It would start with a suspicion, go on to accusations, then counter-accusations, and maybe days of not talking to each other. Each of them is fuming with hard feelings and they don't trust each other anymore.

It will show in everything else they do in school. They would not want to be on the same football team, and each would want to prove their own powers by becoming more influential than the other person. The rivalry only grows, and the environment becomes supportive of the possibility of a big face-off. It can escalate when friends take sides. If parents and teachers have not had a chance to address the underlying issues, it is only a matter of time before the whole thing boils over. What began with Pokémon cards becomes a matter of who will prove themselves right.

Turns out that things get more complicated when problems are between adults, whole communities, and governments. Add uncontrolled power, big ambitions, and weapons at their disposal, and you have trouble waiting to happen! The Second World War can sometimes look like a complex maze, but not to worry. We will understand it well if we pause to put the spotlight on some important happenings. I am sure you will get the hang of the mood and this will help us follow the sequences as they unravel.

Italy

It was the year 1925, and there was a powerful speech given in the Italian Parliament. Benito Mussolini, born to simple parents who worked hard to earn a living, had risen to power a few years back. He was interested in politics from a young age and was curious to know about the affairs of the government. He worked as a journalist for newspapers and ended up clashing with the authorities on many things. He was not afraid of using violence to make his opinions heard and that got him into trouble many times. During the First World War, he promptly joined the Italian army, and after the war, found ways to put pressure on the government through his writings. He was very disappointed with the Treaty of Versailles because he thought it was unfair. Remember

Hitler was also not happy. That smells of a possible future collaboration, doesn't it?

Mussolini believed that Italy needed a dictator with uncontrolled powers if it were to become a strong nation. He started getting many supporters and was notorious for stocking explosives and ammunition in his workplace. The coming years saw him blatantly seizing power to take control of the government. In 1922, he had taken over as the Prime Minister of Italy, but it was his speech in Parliament in 1925 that made it clear to one and all that he would be the supreme leader—a dictator. He became the leader, or Il Duce [say: EEL-DOO-chey] of Italy, which was now a fascist state (you know the definition by now, that's good going!). He made laws that favored his party and anybody who questioned him would be made to suffer. He made sure all the citizens including children were brainwashed into supporting his views. They had to join groups that trained them to think a certain way, the news was controlled and anyone could be arrested for questioning his policies. Well, as suspected, he became pals with Hitler.

(Members of Mussolini's Fascist Party marched on Rome, Oct. 28, 1922)

He watched as Hitler rose to power, and in 1939, Italy and Germany signed a pact called The Pact of Steel, thus giving birth to the Axis. Japan would join the pact in the coming year, sealing the deal for coming together to conquer the world, or so they thought.

Japan

In the meantime, in faraway Japan, a lot was happening. It was a powerful and ambitious empire going about conquering foreign provinces one after the other. As the country started progressing, it wanted to be as powerful as Europe and America. It had old rivalries with China, which was a massive country. Japan's full-scale invasion of China in 1937 was an important trigger for the Second World War. China got support from the Soviet Union and the United States to ward off the enemy. During the onset of the war, Japan went on a conquering spree in the Asian continent. It annoyed France and Britain in the process of taking over their colonies in Asia.

They were in constant conflict with the United States for decades because both had their eyes on ruling over other regions. Japan used to buy a lot of materials like iron, steel, and oil from America. During the war, when Japan began attacking British-owned territories and joined hands with Germany and Italy, it became clear that the United States would do anything to stop Japan. Business stopped between the two countries and both sides tried hard to negotiate and come to agreements, but nothing seemed to work. The second war saw Japan go into massive aggression by launching attacks in all possible directions, and they had a lot of initial victories. However, the stories of cruel treatment of their prisoners of war still gives us goosebumps. Later on, it became impossible for them to keep up with the economic and technological advancement of America, and they started losing out.

The Pearl Harbor surprise attack by Japan is one of the most talked about events in history, and we will revisit it in detail later on. Japan is one country that has lived through the agony of having not one, but two atomic bombs being dropped on its people. It bears sad evidence of the dread that can result when the human race resorts to using weapons capable of destroying the planet.

Germany

Germany's woes were at their heights after the First World War ended in 1918. People had no jobs or money and everyone was desperate. Can you imagine a life with no food to eat and no medicines available when you are sick? Nobody could dream of getting a good education or having fun even once in a while. When Adolf Hitler came along with a promise to help the country out of this misery, he naturally got a lot of support. In 1934 he declared himself the supreme leader, the Führer [say: FYOOR-ER]. He was a different kind because he was obsessed with the idea of "pure" German blood. He put the notion in people's minds that the German or the Aryan race had to thrive and that war was the only way to gain physical space. He began to implement his plans by secretly building an army, even though Germany had promised by signing the treaty that it would not do so.

With a dream of establishing superiority, Germany became the ground for what will remain the most horrible of human tragedies ever to be seen in civilization. The land saw the lives of tens of millions of innocent men, women, and children being snuffed out with nobody to stop Hitler. It churns our stomachs to this day, and we still are baffled at how it even happened.

Germany also started to send troops to attack neighboring countries. Europe was already exhausted from the first war, and countries like Britain and France took their time to respond. Eventually, everyone got pulled in trying to save themselves from the joint aggression of Germany and Italy. After gaining confidence in having captured many countries, Hitler set his eyes on the Soviet Union. After all, it was a large mass of land that would enable the "superior race" to thrive. His dreadful plan of finishing off the Jewish community throughout German-occupied Europe was very much in place.

The invasion of the Soviet Union, however, proved very costly for the German army, and they saw themselves get battered. The Battle of Stalingrad was a fierce combat where Germany tasted big-time defeat. In the meantime, The United States, being the most advanced country at the time, got actively pulled into the war because of its problems with Japan. They had teamed with the Allies and this meant trouble for the Axis. By 1944 the Allied powers had succeeded in invading Germany, and the Soviet Union army entered Germany in 1945. This finally declared Hitler's defeat, and he committed suicide inside his bunker before he could be captured.

(World War 2, Battle of Berlin, May 1945.)

Battlelines Are Drawn at a Feverish Pace

We now have a sense of what the pulse was like in the three countries that made up the Central Axis' major participants at the time (G.I.Joe, help me remember the names of those countries, more ideas, anyone?) So here we are, in the Second World War, the Axis called out the first war cries and The Allies responded.

Now in war and politics, remember that there are no permanent friends or enemies. Strange, but true! Don't be surprised to see countries that are at each other's throats at one particular time, could have been once-upon-a-time besties, or could be so in a faraway future. It usually does not happen during an ongoing war, but we should not be surprised if it does. You see, it's the "enemy's enemy, my friend"; "friend's enemy, my enemy" complications! We can safely say that nobody likes war. It is a last resort because even winning means going through a lot of loss and sadness in the process. Conflicts can happen when people miscalculate the reasons for their difficulties. Just think about believing that my friend complained to the teacher, so I go about making them miserable, only to find out later that it was my misconception?

We will talk a lot about what happened during the world war. At the same let us remember that wars are still an exception. They happen when there is a combination of factors: bad leadership, old hatred, unemployment, or weapons available are just some examples. We seem to have learned our lessons from the past and so the world is better prepared. We are getting better at compromising, cooperating, and being strategic than ever before. Peace talks happen all the time, and they work well. On television, you may have noticed diplomatic meetings and leaders traveling to meet each other. It's just that negative things grab our attention more.

When understanding the world war, we also need to keep in mind that many battles happening at different places, and many incidents happening at different corners, together make up the story of a great war. When we look at events after they happened, we find it easy to pass our judgments, we think, But how could they do that? However, the people out there, leading or fighting, had to make decisions on the go, as they fought, and as they saw people around them suffering or dying. The outcomes of every battle and idea were unpredictable and would take them by surprise. We can only try and imagine what they went through, and learn the lessons that will aid us to negotiate our own lives sensibly.

A Series of Conquests Gain Pace

In Germany, Hitler is confident that his plans will work well. In 1938, he sent an army to attack Austria and then Czechoslovakia. The victories give him even more encouragement,

Adolf Hitler am Deutschen Tag in Hof

since he notices that the major powers at that time, Britain, France, the Soviet Union, and the United States, were busy with their problems and were not paying much attention. In 1939, he signed a pact with the Soviet Union to ensure that they didn't resist his plan of invading Poland. His following invasion of Poland saw it split between Germany and the Soviet Union. This worried Britain and France, and they declared war against Germany. Germany went on to invade Norway, Belgium, and the Netherlands, eventually reaching France. After managing to gain control of a part of France,

Germany directs its attack on Britain.

German planes continued a series of bombings in major locations of Britain from mid-1940 to well into 1941. The "Blitz", or lightning attacks by the Germans, resulted in the deaths of civilians and important places getting destroyed. Britain finally manages to stop the attacks when the British Air Force defeats the German Air Force. By then Britain also began to receive help from the United States, which sent tons of weapons and food in ships across the Atlantic.

Bulgaria, Hungary, and Romania joined the Axis, and Yugoslavia and Greece also came under German control. In 1942, Hitler ordered a surprise invasion of the Soviet Union with a plan. It was named "Operation Barbarossa". He had no idea that it would later on turn out to be a disastrous one. The Soviet Union hit back in the Battle of Stalingrad in a fierce fight, and the last of the German soldiers who survived the harsh winter and the combat surrendered.

Italy Begins to Hit Roadblocks

Italy under Benito Mussolini was no less ambitious. His dream was to restore the old grandeur of the Roman empire by increasing Italy's influence over the Balkan regions. He captured many countries such as Libya, Ethiopia, and Greece, and established control over North and East Africa. In 1939, Italy annexed Albania and intervened in the Spanish Civil War. When Mussolini saw that Adolf Hitler was winning all the initial invasions, Italy took Germany's side in 1940 in hopes of becoming more powerful. But by 1943, it was clear that Italy was ill-prepared. They were not able to keep up with the requirements of guns, planes, and other important war equipment. A lot of people began questioning Mussolini's policies, and so there were divided opinions in Italy about important decisions. The fighters lost motivation. In the middle of the war, the Allied Forces began to actively attack Italy to weaken the Axis. In 1943, Italy had to surrender and Mussolini's government fell. He held onto power with Nazi Germany's help, but was ultimately overpowered in a civil war.

Action in Asia

Up until a hundred years ago, it seemed like the world was all about trying to conquer. It's hard to imagine in today's world that the only way to survive was to snatch from others. We must also understand that it was mostly because life was very difficult back then. Neediness was all over and there was no development like today. There were typically a small number of wealthy, powerful families and a large number of poor people in every society. Regardless of whether they were landlords or kings, the rulers always decided how the vast majority lived and what they did. When the rulers made bad decisions, everybody suffered.

Japan suffered a great depression during the 1920s, and there were millions of poor people in the villages. The ruling groups were expected to do something to bring the country out of all the trouble and frustration. Along with developing trade, they also decided to expand their military powers. And thus began their plans to conquer other regions. Europe and America were going about dominating many Asian countries to exploit their rich resources, and Japan thought it is only right that they do so as well. The balance of power had to be maintained. In today's world, we have the freedom of buying and selling goods and services from around the world. But in those days, every powerful country managed their needs from the land they had conquered, so if they needed more, they had to capture more. If you needed more fuel, then you would go after places that had oil. If you needed aluminum, then you would capture places that have it in plenty.

Japan was increasingly becoming a military state, and since the beginning of the century, had gone about colonizing parts of China, Korea, and Taiwan, along with having constant tensions with the Soviet Union. It set its eyes on the British, French, Dutch, and American colonies and used a mixture of trade and military strategies to control these markets. And much like Germany, the temptation to prove that the Japanese were a superior race was also a factor in Japan's quest to control Asia. From the time it joined the Axis, it went on a full-scale offensive in all directions. In the end, it faced united resistance from the Allies and had to surrender.

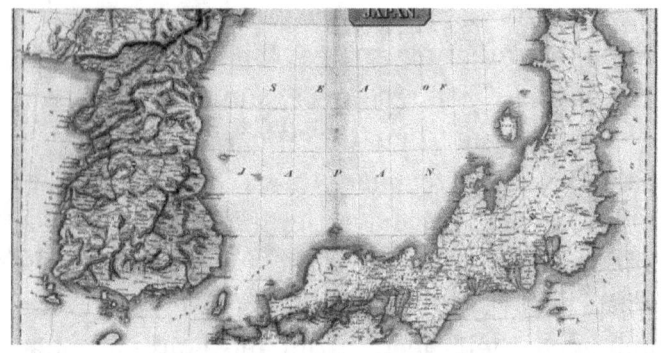

(map of Japan and Korea, showing their geographic proximity)

CHAPTER 3
GETTING MILLIONS OF PEOPLE TO THINK AS THEY DESIRED

• • • • • • • • •

I have a hard time getting my family to agree to see a movie on a Sunday night. I can't help but wonder how lords and despots would influence a whole nation to follow their ideas, whether they were right or wrong. And all that before the days of social media. There was no way of communicating with people as effectively as today. There were no YouTube and Instagram influencers, can you imagine? It is a difficult question, but on close observation, some patterns emerge. The influence was

managed in a very different way. When one group controls all the money, it becomes easier to keep others under their sway. It begins with capturing land and other resources by using brute force, which then converts to money power. Does it work in the modern world? Not very easily because by now society has learned some lessons from the past. We are now quite convinced that violence does not benefit anybody. We are learning to agree amongst ourselves to be fair with one another and have laws to punish anybody who breaks such agreements. Yes, it looks like mistakes are still being made if we were to follow all the bad news we get to watch on television. But we will not give up hope, will we?

Things were, by and large, straightforward in the olden days. Information was controlled by an elite few. Rulers got to decide what the people knew, and what students learned. There was no technology like the internet for people to get independent information. The idea was fed to people that they owed their lives and livelihood to the rulers. Society had strict divisions. Therefore if one was born into a family of farmers, your chances of being a doctor or administrator were pretty slim. The ruling class and rich merchants were the most influential and they got to make all the decisions on who got to do what. The army was trained to follow commands and was strictly under the ruler's authority. The great majority of individuals were laborers who could only obtain compensation by working extremely hard. It appeared to be the same around the world for a very long time.

When Everyone Thinks the Same Way - A Good Thing or Bad?

Social scientists (yes, like science scientists,

there are social scientists, more about them later) love to use the word ideology. What is ideology? Let's see. I have ideas, you have ideas. Ideas about how I should be spending my free time, or when is the right time to chat with friends on Discord. Your mom would have different ideas about the same things. As a family, your parents and siblings, after trials and errors, endless arguments and tears, compromises and smiles, would eventually come to some common agreements on what is acceptable and what is not. You could be happy, or not so happy, with some of them, but a consensus helps in keeping the peace of the house, at least most of the time.

Much like it, the school where you study has agreed upon sets of values that are expected to be respected by everyone, whether you are a teacher, student, or working staff. When it comes to a whole country having a set of values, the process of reaching an agreement becomes more complicated. If half the population believes in something, and the other half has opposite ideas, then we have a big problem. Imagine one half supporting a war and another half not supporting the war. Yet, it is fascinating to be able to understand how a whole country decides to do what it does.

Let us look at how some ideas dominated the minds of people at certain times in history.  Today, when we visit a country and meet its friendly people, it becomes hard to believe that they had a violent or difficult past. We would have read about killings and horrible things that happened in the past, but today the same society would look completely different. How can perfectly normal people behave in unthinkable ways when the situation is different? We will find out more about this, I promise.

Today, we have democracy in most parts of the world. What is democracy? It essentially means that all the people belonging to that country get to choose what kinds of ideas should be used to run their country well. Figuring out what is the best way to run a country will not depend on one person's or group's decision, and everyone will have their say. We will have different political groups, with different ideas, and they will convey them to all the citizens. People will discuss amongst themselves, think about it, observe how the ideas are working, and will then make their choice through the process of elections. Not just that. If at any point you feel the elected leaders are letting you down, you have every right to protest and express your disappointment. Every citizen who is an adult has the right to vote for the leader of their choice. But hey, that does not mean children cannot have an opinion. They can participate by listening keenly, discussing with teachers and parents, and most importantly by listening to all sides of the story. Closing your mind and building prejudices can stop you from making the right decisions. I would say it is better to be confused than to make conclusions about things with the wrong ideas in mind!

But in those days, things were different. Society was not organized like it is today. The people did not have equal status or equal opportunities in anything. Kingship and other high-ranking posts were passed down via the family as an inheritance; utilizing force and might was also an option back then. Such a civilization can be described as an "oligarchy" in our language, where only a small group of wealthy individuals or families have the power to make rules. Everyone was expected to think the same way and agree with the rulers. The problem with such a system was that people in authority would act in ways that were best for themselves rather than considering what was best for everyone. This was because the vast majority of people were underprivileged and unable to stand up for their rights. Things would appear very organized and neat but would end up explosive as a result of all the suppression.

Listening to social scientists is a good idea because they are experts in understanding how human behavior works and how society can be run efficiently. There are never simple answers but it always helps us come to sensible solutions. Their research provides answers to why and how people make decisions, respond to problems, and why things that happened in the past even happened in the first place.

The Japanese Story

Japan is a beautiful country in the far east and is called the Land of the Rising Sun. The Japanese people have a rich culture and are proud of their history. It is a land of great warriors and very hard-working people. Its history dates back a thousand years with emperors ruling the land and the country becoming one of the great powers of the world. Things were, more or less, going fine until Japan began to feel the threat from the Westerners around the beginning of the 1920s. When the interaction and competition with other countries began to increase, the Meiji oligarchs decided that it was best to keep Japan's society strictly organized. They decided that the ruling class had to be able to control the people so that the country could stay united to ward off trouble from foreigners. Now controlling the minds of millions of people is not an easy job. They had to be first convinced of certain thoughts so that they would act according to the wishes of the ruling class.

The first step was to make the emperor a much-feared person. The powerful officers in the palace began expecting people to treat him as a divine being. People were told that he was sacred, and nobody was allowed to take his

name on their lips, or even raise their heads to look at him, and ordinary people weren't able to speak to him. Religious feelings were used to bring a sense of high patriotism to the masses.

It would ultimately mean that people would be willing to lay down their lives for the emperor and the country. So there you go, a sure-shot formula for controlling minds: use fear. Instances of extreme sacrifices for the Emperor became more and more visible in society, and the influence on the minds of the people began getting stronger.

Japan's resentment against the Western world can be in part attributed to challenges in maintaining resources and having equal trading rights, but there was a deeper issue hurting them. It was the question of racial equality. They felt hurt by the taunts of Westerners on many occasions. Some Western nations used racial slurs to put them down despite their accomplishments. When Japan wanted a policy for racial equality in the League of Nations Agreement, it was opposed by Great Britain and America.

The military became extremely strong in Japan in the new order. This was because now the soldiers were highly motivated and ready to go to any length to protect their Emperor and the country's pride. Many of the recruits in the army belonged to villages that were in extreme poverty. It is easy to promise prosperity to someone desperate in exchange for their services in fighting for the nation. The military promised the people that Japan would become the greatest country in the world if they showed their obedience.

The ruling class of Japan also became more and more convinced that democracies in the United States and Great Britain were making the government and its people "soft". They had contempt for freedom of thought. This also became a big reason for their eventual defeat in the Second World War. They became overconfident because they believed that no country could equal their military might. They also believed that it made perfect sense to rule over Asia themselves rather than let the Western countries colonize them. The assumption that they should be the unquestioned lords of Asia attracted animosity from a lot of the surrounding countries. Japan's decision to plunge into the world war was influenced by its perception of racial superiority within Asia, the urge to challenge Western dominance, and its unbridled military power.

But Why Did Japan Attack America?

We understand by now that Japan did not like the Westerners during those times. They wanted to become the most mighty Asian country and hence went about conquering their neighbors. Historians today still discuss if the Pearl Harbor attack on America in 1941 was a good idea. Japan was aware that America was very powerful, and also knew that America was not keen on attacking their land. The United States had more money and military strength. Moreover, Japan was dependent on America for fuel and steel, both of which were important to

run the military. Though America was not keen on confronting Japan directly, it did begin to stop the supply of oil and steel to weaken them in Asia. Japan realized that it could not continue its conquests in Asia without these supplies.

They had to look for solutions to their problems and planned to conquer the Dutch and British colonies of Southeast Asia to have their oil resources. The only problem with this plan was the presence of the American Pacific fleet in the Pacific Ocean. The fleet was stationed close to Japan, at Pearl Harbor, in Hawaii. Japan was, for many reasons, confident that America would not attack them even if this fleet was destroyed, and they launched a surprise attack. It was a gamble they took, but it cost them dearly because they had miscalculated America's response. Japan's military actions invited enmity from the West, as well as within Asia, and the tragic atomic bombings finally led to the country's surrender in the Second World War.

The American Story

It is intriguing to know how the United States got all caught up in the war. Now America was a brand new creation of civilized society. Unlike many parts of the world that carried the burden of thousands of years of civilization, America was built from scratch about 250 years ago by settlers from all over the world. It got to make fresh rules and dream new dreams. America represented the free human spirit because it did not belong to any particular race. It called for its people to have patriotism towards their country, but also laid equal emphasis on individual rights and self-empowerment. America entered the Second World War in 1941, mid-way. But the fact that it was the world's most powerful nation also made its every move significant. It remained neutral for the first two years, but had its sympathies with Britain and France.

As it watched Germany conquer one country after another and pound the Allies, the American government, under President Franklin Roosevelt in 1940, decided to support England by sending army men. America was still not part of the war and was only involved in arming the Allies. The intention was that it would be the savior of democracy in all parts of the world. This angered the German army and triggered their attack on US warships.

As they were keeping a watch on developments in Europe, America was also keenly monitoring Japan's activities. When making decisions, it kept in mind Japan's invasions of China and Manchuria, the European colonies in Asia, and its wars with the Soviet Union. America also saw Japan's activities as a threat to the ideas of democracy. It kept the pressure on Japan by enforcing trade restrictions, and by refusing to sell things that Japan badly needed. Despite these factors, the United States was not keen on a military confrontation until it was jolted by the Pearl Harbor attack. Now war became inevitable with Japan, and on the other side, Germany declared war on the United States.

But then how were the common people of America convinced that they needed to do anything to serve their country? There was no emperor, dictator, or divine entity to be afraid of. But they had the "American way of life" to protect. Public opinion was strong, it mattered, and it would sway with the need of the hour. They were as zealous as the citizens of Japan to lay down their lives to protect the spirit of freedom in their country. As the war went on in Asia and Europe, public opinion began to favor America taking a stand and not just watching from the sidelines. You understand that it is sometimes difficult to just stand and watch when there is an unfair fight going on around you. Would you not want to do something about it? America made great sacrifices and lost half a million soldiers, and by the end of the war rose in status as an undisputed world power, an influencer who dreamt of a democratic world.

(President Franklin Roosevelt)

CHAPTER 4
LIFE ON THE HOMEFRONT

• • • • • • • • • •

But what is it like for the people who live in countries that go to war? They are all people just like you and me, they work to provide for the family, they have dreams, and everyone wants their children, parents, uncles, aunts, cousins, and friends to be happy and safe. But everything seems to turn upside down the moment their government declares that it is wartime now. All of a sudden, people are ordered to join the army, jobs are lost, food runs out, families are forced to flee their homes, and you are asked to forget about your plans. There appears to

be only confusion and chaos left. Can we imagine this happening to us just like that? Unfortunately, things like this have happened and continue to happen in some place or the other. We need to know this so that we don't end up in this situation in the future. When it happens, we need to know what can come out of it.

Now before we get all paranoid and worried, we also need to know how to face situations bravely since that is also part of life. Struggles come to us even during peaceful times. We get sick, we get pulled up for bad behavior, we lose jobs, and we fail exams. Can you make a list of challenges that you have seen people face? It will be a good idea to talk to adults and friends to find out more about their difficulties. The things that happened and what they did to overcome them will surprise you. It will also help to know that there are rules in war too. Nations in the modern world agreed to follow them or otherwise face severe disadvantages once the war is over. Yes, some rules get broken in the chaos, but there is an effort to follow them in general.

What exactly happens when a country is attacked? Let us try and understand this first. The army is the first to face the other because each side is trying to prevent the other from damaging important property. What exactly is an important property? They are military sites, industrial sites that produce all the important stuff, dams, power stations, oil rigs, ships, warehouses that stock goods, and any such place that keeps a country functioning. The people get categorized into the army and civilians. The recruitment into the army increases manyfold. The soldiers have a different experience. These men and women work under orders and are on the frontline taking the maximum impact. Civilians have a different kind of struggle. Old people, women staying back to support the family, and children suffer bad treatment, often with the risk of injury, violence, sickness, and homelessness increasing. I think experiencing these pains will force anyone to look out for ways to coexist peacefully.

Rationing and Shortages

Everything we do would get disturbed if our nation were to go to war. Food is amongst the first things to get erratic. People working on the farms are able-bodied people and they would be the ones asked to enlist in the army. Produce grown on farms would not get to cities on time because transport would be diverted. The government would have to make sure that everyone got food. To make sure that supplies reached the frontlines, as well as civilians, the authorities would enforce rationing. It meant that food items, clothing, paper, rubber, metal, and many other consumer goods would not be available when people needed them. Ration cards and stamps would be issued to every family and one would probably be allowed to buy only four loaves of bread in a week and would be expected to recycle their clothes. Clothes had to be exchanged when children outgrew them and shoes were always in shortage. People would not be able to buy new tires for their cars if the older ones needed replacement. First sugar disappeared from shop shelves, then meat and cheese. Using less was considered a good way of showing patriotism and meant that everyone including very young children did their part in sacrificing for the war. In the United States, citizens were encouraged to have their own vegetable gardens.

Imagine that what we are used to eating in a day or two would be what families in those days stretched for nearly a week. Difficult to even think about, right? In Britain, the Ministry of Food was set up to make sure that everyone followed the food rules. There would be posters  everywhere, television and radio broadcasts to encourage people to cooperate. No one liked the idea of having less, but there was no choice. Everyone was encouraged to look at it as an opportunity to sacrifice for the country. My grandma still hates to waste and has clever hacks to make tasty dishes using very simple ingredients, now I know what led her to it.

Japan introduced strict rationing systems to control its people. There were times when these rations would not reach them, which made them desperate and resort to theft. Production was completely controlled by the government, and at times the production of important items like textiles would be completely stopped for long periods. Children as young as twelve would be expected to work after their school hours and life was very hard. The rationing system also had many problems. People would try to cheat. There was a "black market" where things were illegally sold, and some people would get exploited. Criminal activities were on the rise since it was difficult to keep a check on everything. Societies had to suffer the indirect effects of war as well.

It was not just the countries that were at war that had to face shortages. Many regions that were thousands of miles away and had nothing to do with the war also saw death, hunger, and untold misery. These countries would be under the rule of the nations that were directly involved in the war and they would simply order that men, food, and other supplies came from these places. Millions of families in India and Southeast Asia have gone hungry because food would be shipped from their farms to feed the armies in Europe, and thousands have lost their lives from faraway lands as a direct impact of the war.

Propaganda and Censorship

Propaganda is perhaps the most sensitive and intriguing topic to speak about. It is the process of getting certain ideas into people's minds and getting them to act the way you want them to. Governments and leaders, kings and priests, have used it throughout history. It is a double-edged sword. It can help when used for the right cause, but do unimaginable harm when done for selfish motives. During World War II, there was a flood of propaganda happening on all fronts.

In the Western world, the popular image of Japan was that its people could be effortlessly motivated to give their lives for the country. We had films made in America about how the Japanese were uniformly a brutal race, and the Japanese people in turn were fed news about how the Westerners were arming themselves to attack them.

The truth of the matter was that, very much like the Nazis of Germany, the Japanese government had to constantly persuade and use force to get the people to agree to their plans. The reality was that convincing a nation to be the aggressor is more challenging than calling upon people to defend the country.

Brainwashing the minds of a whole society is a very carefully planned and deliberate effort spread over some time. It is not easy to convince you and me to attack another person. I would naturally be more interested in living happily and keeping my family safe, rather than thinking of dying for an unknown cause.

Let us see what happens. Certain patterns are followed by the group that is interested in swaying the minds of people in a certain direction. The first step would be to build fear. I am interested in my happiness, so I need to begin to see a threat in that.

Information has to be controlled (in other words, censored) so that nobody has a chance to see different sides of the story. So the reports in the newspapers, radio, and television are checked and modified before they are broadcast, and textbooks have material that suits the rulers and does not allow children to think freely. This will gradually lead to everyone thinking, talking, and behaving in a certain uniform way. It is all good if it was being done to teach good things, like being kind and courteous, but if it was being done to convince a community to hate another community so much as to be able to kill it, it is nothing but a great disservice to humanity. It could fetch short-term results, but in the long term, it would only make the world a terrible place.

Japanese leaders had a tough job in hand. They were keenly watching Hitler in Germany and taking inspiration for mobilizing their people through persuasion and force, but unlike Germany, they did not have the money and technology to effectively market their plans. It is much like selling products today, I guess.  Spend a lot of money on some awesome advertising campaigns, and voila, the product sells like hotcakes. Most of the population in Japan were poor and illiterate and did not have radios like many in Germany. So reaching out through media or newspapers was not an option.

But the military began a National Spiritual Mobilization Campaign to influence the thoughts of people. They made memberships compulsory and began to push the idea of patriotism by showing pictures of young people in military uniforms and saving the country. It became easier to organize rallies that spoke of crushing foreign countries to save Japan. Children in school were taught to be obedient to the Emperor. All Western ideas were rejected in the name of restoring Japanese culture. Force could be used rather easily because people had no power.

Internment of Japanese-Americans

As we learned, America is a nation built by people from all over the world who settled there and made it their home. It had its problems in dealing with racism and the challenges of white domination. Discriminating laws were being enacted with majority votes. But on the other hand, America also dreamt of becoming a great country with equal opportunities for everyone. Along with having Europeans, Africans, and people from literally every corner of the world settled in the land for a long time, this meant that it had a good number of Japanese-origin citizens too. Almost a hundred years before the Second World War, millions of Japanese families had migrated from the Empire of Japan in search of jobs. Many of them had settled in the United States and got American citizenship. They had gotten jobs and were working hard to earn a living.

When tensions with Japan started rising, the United States government kept a close watch on the Japanese settlements with the help of military intelligence. They did not find any activities amongst the community where they could be accused of disloyalty to the country. This suddenly changed when Japan attacked Pearl Harbor. The Japanese- Americans began to be seen as people belonging to an enemy country, and during the period of the war more than one million Japanese descendants were forcibly relocated to places that were marked as imprisonment camps. The mood became heavy overnight and the Japanese Americans lost their jobs, school and college admissions, friends, and homes. They were looked upon with suspicion everywhere they went. They were interned, that is, confined, like prisoners, and lived in concentration camps set up by the American government. People would be asked many questions by the authorities to test their loyalty to America and would be sent to different camps depending on the answers. Wait to hear of the unique role Japanese Americans played in the war; that of utmost sacrifice and loyalty in the face of mistrust and discrimination!

Life in the Camps

When families get affected, it means no one escapes the disturbances, including young children and old people. Families got separated because they were taken to different locations and they were made to live in camps on grounds that were surrounded by barbed wires. The quarters were very tiny with no washrooms or kitchens. The role of fathers and mothers also changed. Parents could not take care of their children because they were required to do long hours of work. This was hard on the minds of everyone.

They all ate from a common kitchen with no choices in food. The ventilation was poor, bathrooms were shared, laundry could not be done, and diseases were breaking out because of these conditions. They lived in these tough circumstances without any freedom for around four years. People suffered because of a lack of medical facilities, emotional stress, and unfair treatment, the memories stayed long after the war was over.

There was tension within the families because now they were expected to behave differently, and they could not understand why their lives were getting so disturbed. When fathers were taken away as prisoners, the other family members, including children, would have to take the responsibility of working and earning for the family.

In the camps, the internees were not initially paid for working, but this changed later. The quality of their lives naturally went down and they were only doing jobs that kept the concentration camps running. People got odd jobs that were mostly not connected with their qualifications. Teaching, writing for camp newspapers, keeping shop, accounting, and administrative jobs were for people with skills, while the others got construction, maintenance, and cleaning work. Agriculture and animal herding were also done to grow food. They would also be taken out of the camps to work on farms and mills whenever there would be a labor shortage.

After about five years the camps finally began closing down due to government orders. The thousands of people who came out of the camps found it very difficult to start life afresh because they had lost their previous jobs and houses.

Lessons to Learn

We don't know if that was the right thing to do, but the American government made those decisions as part of security measures, and also perhaps to put pressure on Japan. Lives got upset for nobody's fault. Do you think it is fair if you are forced to move out of your home because you look a certain way? It is a situation where the people who force others also repent of such decisions. War is hard on everyone. Forty years after the war was over the American government officially apologized to the incarcerated families because they realized that it was an unfair thing to happen.

The lesson we learn is that during wars decisions are sometimes taken based on hysteria, racism, and popular sentiment. After the war is over, we feel bad and regret things that get done and just have to live with the wrongs that happened. This is the tragedy of war. You would probably agree that it is better to do everything needed to prevent a war, including knowing more about each other's problems, thinking about different possible solutions, talking to each other calmly, and agreeing on compromises. Don't we have that choice?

CHAPTER 5
TURNING POINTS OF THE WAR

• • • • • • • • • •

Invasion of Poland, but Why?

If someone has savage plans in mind, how do they go about doing what they want to? By resorting to bullying and lying in the least. That is exactly what Hitler did. He thought that the 'pure' German race needed more land to live and thrive. Poland was the neighbor. He decided that the Poles were inferior people who could only be used for serving the Germans, and of course, they had no right to have a country of their own. He had to take ownership. But how do you attack your neighbor just like that? Spread a lie. He got some Germans to dress up as Poles and attack German property.

(German soldiers invade Poland)

He announced on national radio that Poland had attacked Germany and used propaganda to convince the Germans that Poles were out to harm them. Thus, on September 1st, 1939, the

German army sprung into action and pounded Poland, in violation of all previously agreed positions. They bombed important places and many thousands of Polish people lost their lives. To add to the agony, on September 17th, the Soviet Union attacked Poland from another side. The brave people gave their everything to defend their nation, but stood no chance at the double attack. There was no way it could defend itself against two powerful countries for long, and Poland surrendered in about a month. About seven million people in Poland lost their lives in the course of the occupation.

To Hitler's mind, Poland was just a stepping stone because it was a smaller nation with a weaker army. After all, countries like Poland, Czechoslovakia, Austria, and Hungary, among others, were new nations born after Germany's humiliating defeat in the First World War. Germans were living in those countries, and it became an excuse for Hitler to get them back into Germany's fold. The idea was to take control of the whole of Europe.

As we know, Britain and France already had an understanding after the First World War that they would come to Poland's help in case it was attacked. They kept their promise and declared war on Germany. But as Hitler had rightly calculated, they would be too slow and weak in their responses. The Allies underestimated Hitler's moves and were caught unprepared. On the other hand, the Russians and the Germans were also traditional enemies. But, interestingly, they had signed a pact where they promised not to attack each other. It also included a secret promise that they would equally divide nations that lay between them. Poland was one such nation, and so when it was attacked by Germany, the logical step by the Soviet Union was to take its share of the country. It attacked Poland to get its share of the kill as the world watched in shock.

There was also another reason for other countries of the world not responding fast enough to Germany's unreasonable behavior. After bearing the loss of lives in the First World War, nobody was in the mood for another round. All they wanted was to be able to rebuild their nations. Since Poland was already defeated, there was nobody they had to rush to save. Hitler was cunning enough to see the opportunities that were coming his way and he got bolder. While everyone was hoping that the crisis would die down, Germany trained its guns toward France next. That is when Europe woke up to the bitter fact that it would take another full-blown war to stop Hitler. On May 10th,

1940, Hitler's army reached France and in little over a month entered Paris and successfully captured it. The Allies consisting of Britain, France, Belgium, Luxemburg, and the Netherlands were unprepared this time too.

Battle of Britain

Less than a year after they set foot out of Germany, Hitler's army had Poland, Norway, Belgium, Denmark, the Netherlands, Luxembourg, and France under their control. The German Army used tactics known as the Blitzkrieg, or lightning attack, to take control of opposing armies. They would use quick-moving tanks and air force support to cut through the enemy ranks and surround them. It was time to look towards Britain. The Nazis had a lot of confidence in themselves by this point and thought Britain would be an easy victory. They began Operation Sea Lion (the code name for the attack on Britain). The German army realized that their main challenge was the British Royal Air Force

and the Battle of Britain was essentially a war in the skies. On July 10th, 1940 the Luftwaffe, the German Air Force, went in for their first attack. They continued bombing the British airstrips and industrial areas to gain control. In a few weeks, they realized outwitting them was going to be more difficult than they assumed. Britain's responses were strong and devastating for the Germans. They changed their strategy and resorted to targeting civilians and began regular bombings of London City. By May 1941 the Germans realized that it was taking them nowhere and they finally had to abandon their plans of capturing Britain, at least for the moment. The Battle of Britain turned out to be Germany's first taste of failure since they had begun their trial of devastation. Hitler decided to concentrate on the East for now. After all, the Soviet Union needed to be under German control for many reasons, the most important being that Germany needed more land for their race to flourish. Hitler hated the ideas of the Communist Russian government led by dictator Stalin in any case.

Invasion of the Soviet Union and the Battle of Stalingrad

On June 22nd, 1941, the German army launched its attack on the Soviet Union under the name Operation Barbarossa. All the while Hitler kept the motivation of his army and citizens high with his fiery speeches and propaganda where he continued convincing them that they were the most superior people in the world and had to get the entirety of Europe under their control. But now, as we see it, the Russian invasion was a massive mistake that cost Hitler dearly. The Russians were taken by surprise because they did not expect Germany to break the non-aggression pact. The German army was quite successful in the initial days and managed to reach Leningrad which was deep inside Soviet territory. They went about killing people who they thought were racially inferior. There were all possibilities that Germany would succeed in its plan of taking over the country. But the Soviet army was really large and was preparing itself for a counterattack. Four months into the war, the German army began to show signs of exhaustion. They were not prepared for the winter and tough landscapes. Towards the end of 1941, the Russians gathered their wits back and struck back with vengeance. The painful battles went on for some time.

(German soldiers at a grave)

On August 23rd, 1942, the German army launched an attack to encircle the city of Stalingrad in southwest Russia, and this turned out to be easily the most brutal of battles in the history of wars. They were getting pounded by the Russian army but did not get permission from Hitler to retreat or surrender. The ordeal finally ended on February 2nd, 1943 when Germany finally accepted defeat. The Soviet Union paid a heavy price by having the most number of casualties in the entire war. Can you believe that of the one hundred thousand German army men who were at the site of the battle of Stalingrad, only about six thousand returned to Germany? About nine thousand people lost their lives in the battle and about ninety thousand more army men died due to falling sick, being exhausted, and lack of food. Apart from this crushing defeat, the whole episode made the Allies stronger. Even though Britain and the Soviet Union were not friends, they joined together to keep Germany in control.

D-Day Invasion

If the Allies were caught unprepared in 1939, they were gradually but surely preparing their moves. Winston Churchill, the Prime Minister of the United Kingdom, and Franklin D Roosevelt, the President of the United States, had set upon themselves to defeat the Axis powers at any cost. The Allies took their time to prepare defenses, understand their advantages, and figure out what Hitler could be thinking. In the summer of 1944, they finally thought themselves ready to take on Germany. The first move was made on June 6th, 1944 by landing over a hundred and fifty-six thousand troops on the shores of Normandy. The goal was to take charge of German-occupied France which came to be known as the D-Day invasion, a turning point for the Allies. They started to make small but definite progress and succeeded in pushing back the German troops. At the same time, the Russians, who had by now joined the Allies, began pushing back the Germans from the east by launching Operation Bagration. Hitler's Germany was being attacked from the East and

West at the same time. The United States was also active in the war by now which gave the Allies a much-needed boost.

The D-Day invasion turned out to be an epic move. It was one of the toughest because of the stormy weather on the shores of Normandy and the German resistance worked strongly against them. Hitler miscalculated because of his overconfidence and the deception unit of the Allies, about whom you will read later. It followed a counter-attack from Germany's side in the fierce Battle of the Bulge and the Allies once again won. Germany was preparing itself for an attack and so the Allies did not expect things to be easy for them. But it was nail-biting, complete with spies, double agents, and landing with inflatable docks on shores without a port—maneuvers that would make thrilling movies.

Attack on Pearl Harbor, December 7th, 1941

Right in the middle of the massive Pacific Ocean, somewhat at an equal distance from both Japan and the mainland of the United States, lies a teeny-weeny cluster of islands almost invisible when you look at the world map. Something that happened there changed the world order forever. The Hawaiian Islands is a state of the United States, though physically located really far away.

What prompted Japan to provoke the more powerful United States is being debated even today, but the truth is that it did. As we learned, tensions between the countries were already simmering ever since Japan got ambitious in colonizing countries in Asia. The European powers and the United States felt that it would threaten their markets and their influence on the world order. They responded by making it difficult for Japan to sell and buy goods needed to run the country and, obviously, Japan thought it was unfair to be bullied by the West and was not happy with this situation. When things were getting heated up, the Japanese government decided to take a risk. They decided to attack the United States military base in the Hawaiian Islands so that there would be no resistance to its plans to capture more parts of Southeast Asia. They calculated that the United States would not bother to come after them.

Pearl Harbor was a naval base with warships, aircraft, and military men stationed on the island. In a normal war situation, there is a declaration of war and the United States would have known that Japan was preparing an attack. But the Japanese decided to make this a surprise attack, which in principle is not a fair thing to do. What do you think? But there are sometimes no rules in war, much as everyone tries. Unfortunately, it becomes all about winning, by hook or by crook, only to pay the price later!

On an early Sunday morning, December 7th, 1941, a usual rest day for the United States military, Japanese fighter aircraft swept into the Hawaiian skies and dropped bombs one after the other. In the next two hours, more than a dozen navy ships were damaged or sunk, and more than two thousand people were killed with more than a thousand injured. The United States, until then a neutral country in the Second World War, decided to plunge head-on into the war. We know what happens when a giant gets into a fight; the consequences are not small. Four years after the Pearl Harbor attack,

Japan surrendered after the United States dropped two atomic bombs, killing more than two hundred thousand people and causing long-term effects on the Japanese people and the land.

CHAPTER 6
THE HOLOCAUST

Surely none of us like the idea of dying. The thought of death makes us feel scared, sad, hopeless, and pessimistic, and therefore we don't want to even talk about it. But the thing is that death is as real as life. Let us muster some courage and spend some time talking about it. Death is a mystery that people have been trying to solve forever. Did you know that many civilizations give a lot of importance to the subject, and sometimes even celebrate death because it is, after all, the truth of life? Deaths happen, and whole species vanish when the environment changes. Diseases, accidents, old age, and natural calamities cause deaths. We find it easier to accept natural deaths. What can be mind-boggling is death caused on purpose, where people kill others for selfish reasons. How do we reconcile to such events?

(Auschwitz)

The time of World War II also saw the tragic murder of around six million European Jews. We know it as the Holocaust. It is a difficult catastrophe to accept, we don't want to believe that it even happened. How was it possible for one man to decide that killing people would solve his problems, and how did he get other people to follow his plans? Surely there is something more to it. We need to know so that we don't get ourselves into such a situation ever again.

What Caused The Hatred?

Let's dig a little deeper to understand the situations that lead to the Holocaust. The sentiment against the Jewish community in Europe was negative for a long long time, going back to the middle ages. The discrimination is rooted in religion because they were held responsible for the death of Christ. For hundreds of years, a lot of professions were banned for them, Jews were not allowed to own properties in good parts of the town, and they would be targeted whenever there were problems, and were even accused of causing the plague many centuries ago. In those days people used to look at each other based on the race they belonged to, and lived with the idea that nations belonged to certain races and not others. Think of being unliked because you belonged to a certain place, and looked a certain way. We are learning to overcome this kind of thinking. How fair do you think it is?

Talking about preferences, we like certain things and dislike others at different points in life, right? I remember the times I hated eggplants and wished there were no eggplants in the world. I love them now because my tastes have evolved and I understand their importance. It would have been such a tragedy if my wish of vanishing eggplants had come true. It holds for any idea in the world. We end up doing things that are unacceptable and notice that it starts with seemingly harmless feelings. It sometimes begins with fear, and sometimes with a feeling of superiority over the other. We forget that we have no right to decide whether another being exists or not. Co-existence is a humane way of living, it is the ideal we aspire for. Otherwise, beginning with dislike, it leads to disrespect, and disgust, and ends with a crime. We cross all boundaries especially when we have the power to do so.

When the First World War ended, some groups in Germany blamed the Jews for it and were not ashamed of expressing their hatred for the Jewish community. The Nazis became very powerful and circumstances led them to take

extreme measures during the war. They thought that taking harsh actions was the only way to get their plans to succeed. The decision of engaging in mass murders came from a combination of hatred and the need to do something effective enough to retain power.

The Nazis made life difficult for the Jews in Germany and there were a lot of criminal activities targeting them, but eliminating the entire community was initially not in their minds. During the initial days, Jews were encouraged or forced to migrate out of the country. The 1930s were the most difficult for them. There were restrictions on jobs and entry to public spaces like parks and eateries. Inter-race marriages were prohibited by law and they became second-class citizens with limited rights. In 1938, the Nazi party organized violence against the Jews by destroying their property and attacking their places of worship. Thousands of them were imprisoned in concentration camps and it became really bad when the war broke out in 1939. The Nazis began to execute Jews in Poland and the Soviet Union when they captured these countries. They made sure the living conditions of Jews were bad so that survival would be difficult.

What Makes Normal People Do Cruel Acts?

We all know that the German army and officials worked on strict orders to indulge in acts of killing innocent people. But isn't it puzzling how they could be convinced to do such things? Perhaps some of them were criminal-minded and motivated by the greed of having Europe for their race. But the mass murders were systematically done across places and for a sustained period. The people who executed the orders were ordinary people; they were educated, modern men and women. They did horrible acts because they were given no choice and did what they were told out of their sense of duty. Thinking back, the actions of people also depend on the information that is fed to them. Today, news spreads in a matter of seconds. Wrong news spreading will surely get us into trouble, but the good news now is that the right information also spreads equally fast. We can lay our hands on both sides of the story and decide what we need to do. Imagine a situation where only wrong news spread because that team was more powerful, more organized, and they controlled the sources of the news. Precious time gets lost before the truth comes out. By then too many people are brainwashed and too many wrong actions are done before people realize the truth.

Conflict can make us do strange things. It is as if chance decides on which side we fall and this makes it difficult for us to judge people for what they do. They did what they did just because they had a dictator who had uncontrolled powers to do what he willed. They have had to live the rest of their life in regret and the traumatic memories of what they did during the war. Unthinkable, isn't it? There have been many studies done to understand what goes on in the minds of people when they end up doing things they would never otherwise do. Scientists and doctors who study behavior found that creating certain social situations can change the way people respond. We cross lines that separate good from evil when we are put in environments that foster negativity.

Stanley Milgram, a social psychologist, used an electric shock experiment to demonstrate how people could be persuaded to commit wrongdoing. In the experiment, he encouraged one group of people to administer a mild electric shock to another group. He gradually increased the intensity of the shock and was intrigued at how the first group showed willingness in inflicting pain. Brainwashing led the pain givers to think they were helping instead of hurting. The results revealed some important things that will help us recognize them. Usually, the person or group would work hard to put an idea in our minds, then you would be made to do small tasks that would look innocent, they would convince you to feel powerful by doing so, and they would keep you occupied with ever-changing plans. Have you noticed that bullies behave similarly? They like to label others as bad, which makes it easier for them to go after them. Many similar experiments have helped us identify a lot of such patterns where we tend to pick up prejudices easily.

(Auschwitz)

Catch Them Young

If you notice, most people who want to influence others target young people for brainwashing. The Nazis did it and so does any organization that wants a community to think in a certain way. It is therefore extremely useful to look at anything with a healthy amount of doubt, no matter who is trying to impose their opinion. It could be someone on social media, experts, or even friends and family. If such influences are having an impact on our own life, it will be useful to pause and reflect. Take your time to learn more about it, think of the intention behind the opinion, get opposing viewpoints, and experiment with different possibilities. We need to be aware that people are constantly attempting to sway one another. Companies try to persuade us that purchasing their product is so important for us, political leaders attempt to persuade the public to accept their viewpoints, and friends sometimes persuade us to pull practical jokes on others. I believe it's critical to see the patterns and to constantly be able to reason for oneself.

What Went on in the Extermination Camps

Gila was eight years old and living in a quaint little village in Poland. Her days began and ended prancing around a farm full of chickens, ponies, and fish in the ponds. Her grandfather managed the large farm and her dad was studying in England to be a lawyer. Her life changed just like that when one afternoon some people knocked on their door and marched them off to a concentration camp. She lived till eighty and grew up to be a brave woman who rebuilt her life in faraway America since she was one of the few lucky ones who survived thanks to a Nazi officer's kind wife who secretly sheltered her. But the trauma of seeing cruelty stayed with her and haunted her for the rest of her life. She recalls how until that tragic day her family was uprooted from their home, she only had happy memories of her childhood. She had not sensed any hatred or discrimination in the community for being Jewish.

For us and future generations, the Nazi concentration camp will forever be symbolic of human evil and mass murder. More than a thousand camps and sub-camps were run by Nazi Germany to carry out its "racial cleansing" program for around nine years, ending in 1945. They used it as a way of maintaining fear and eventually eliminating everyone they felt did not belong to their land. They used all their might to build this alien idea into society. Their main targets were the Jews but also included other minority groups, differently-abled people, criminals, and political opponents. It was a strange and frightening idea that seemed to be brought to reality. It was as if Hitler and his group thought they would decide who had the right to live and who did not. Their cruelty did not spare the Germans either. More than a hundred thousand Germans were killed secretly when they were found to be physically or mentally disabled. The camps were organized and run by the SS, a semi-military group controlled by Hitler and the Nazi party. Since the Nazis believed that they needed to watch out for enemies within Germany, they were continuously active in spying on and punishing people who stood up against them. The number of prisoners massively increased in the later years as the war progressed.

Normally when people are sent to prisons as punishment, basic living conditions are taken care of. Food, hygiene, medical care, clothing, and such needs for living with dignity are not denied. They lose their freedom no doubt, but they are not left to die. The concentration camps were different because the people who were running the camps did not want their prisoners alive. Millions of people died because they were exhausted by forced labor, starved, or inflicted by contagious diseases that spread in the unhealthy conditions of the camp. All this happened even though there was a rule against conducting inhuman acts during the war under the Hague Convention, signed by nations way back in 1907.

The confined people were used as free labor in farms, construction areas, quarries, and factories making war equipment and as domestic help in the officer residences. Things got worse when the planned killing of prisoners began. It started by killing sick and tired prisoners who were not capable of doing labor work. In the following years, Soviet prisoners of war were executed. They began to use poisonous gas to cause death. The use of gas chambers began to increase with hundreds of people being killed at the same time. The Auschwitz camp in Poland is remembered in history as the deadliest site of all.

What about the large number of Nazi and SS members who carried out the cruel orders given to them? How did they act in such unimaginable ways? They were all people who had no jobs and no money. They were promised a salary and comfortable living if they joined the party. They were not in a position to choose because they had a dictator ruling them. The officers who did the job were perhaps brainwashed to think that they were helping the prisoners out of suffering. As we read about the behavioral science experiment done by scientists, it would have been easy to influence their minds. The ordinary people in Germany were regularly fed news that supported the Nazi ideas and were made to believe that what was happening was for the good of the country. Even if the reality of the concentration camps shocked them, they could not freely express their opinion.

CHAPTER 7
END OF WAR

• • • • • ● • • •

If you can remember the full sequence, the last face-off with your friend or sibling started full throttle, continued for a while with earnestness, and somewhere down the road began to show signs of waning. However long the tiff lasted, somewhere down the line decisions began to get influenced by a lot of things. People around would have begun to notice, suggestions and advice would begin to pour into your ears, and you would begin to have second thoughts. You would become wiser and begin to start looking at the problem in another way, or one of the sides would have such powerful advantages that the other side would have no choice but to surrender.

(damage in London)

Similarly, the countries bashing each other began showing signs of reaching some conclusion. The World War peaked in the first few years of the 1940s and patience began wearing thin. Each side needed to do something to quicken the end game. The Axis had only two fighting players left. It was now about Germany and Japan up against the whole world. America's entry with its powerful weapons began to influence the war more than anything else. The Allied forces got stronger because they were united, became better at understanding the enemies, and began to break enemy codes and use innovation. Let us zoom into the year 1945 and follow it closely to fully understand the dramatic turns.

The Battle of Berlin and the V-E Day

For Germany, everything after D-Day was chaos. They found themselves being attacked aggressively by the Allies from all directions. They were running short of resources and showing signs of strain. The Axis powers realized they were losing the war. Italy, which had been reduced to being a puppet of Nazi Germany, gets pushed over by the Allies. In January 1945, the Allied troops finally succeeded in getting inside Germany from the western side because of the heavy firebombing in certain German cities. Streets were literally being set on fire, and there was devastation everywhere. Meanwhile, the Soviet troops were coming down heavily from the eastern side and they successfully entered the capital of Poland, liberated it from the Germans, and continued marching toward the heart of Germany. The Soviet troops launched their battle against Berlin, the capital city, to encircle it. The Battle of Berlin, which lasted a fortnight, ended when the Russians stormed Berlin, thus symbolizing the capture of Nazi Germany and putting an end to the tragic saga.

April 1945 turned out to be the month of the grand finale. Hitler shot himself to death in his bunker on April 30th, 1945, before he could be captured. Two days prior, his friend Benito Mussolini was executed in Italy. Germany surrendered to the Allies, and May 8th is marked as Victory in Europe Day, also known as the V-E Day. It was a day of great celebrations, especially in the United States, Canada, the United Kingdom, and France, while The Soviet Union celebrates its Victory Day on May 9th. The world heaved a sigh of relief. But wait, things in the Pacific Theater, the area of ocean and islands in the Pacific, had yet to reach closure.

Dropping The Atomic Bomb and the V-J Day

The Pacific Theater was having more trouble bringing things to an end. Japan was fighting with all its might and appeared adamant about not giving up. The islands of Japan were still witnessing fierce battles with thousands from each side dying every single day. Unfortunately, they had no clue that the United States was losing patience and was busy with some super top-secret projects up its sleeve.

The United States was a fertile ground for innovation because it had brilliant people settled there from all over the world, and it had a thriving economy compared to the rest of the world. To add to the energy, many of the people were refugees who had fled the war. They had a strong motivation to do anything to stop the forces that had caused them so much pain. The government began to look for scientists, mathematicians, and people with creative ideas. Top-secret projects began to take shape that aimed at building weapons to take the enemies by surprise. Something interesting was forming. It was a monster that the world had never imagined and it was as if mankind had caught hold of something supernatural. It was the atomic bomb, born of nuclear science. On the day it was put to the test, those in attendance experienced extreme joy and unrelenting anguish, its potential to destroy would haunt them for the rest of their lives. The environment appeared to change from darkness to dazzling sunshine. Oppenheimer, the brilliant scientist known as the father of the atomic bomb, described how he could hear the words, "Now I have become death, the destroyer of worlds," from the sacred Bhagwad-Gita when he witnessed its testing. The atomic bombs were ready to be deployed whenever needed. The Allies asked Japan to surrender unconditionally, as the months of fighting were dragging on, but it refused and continued to hold the fort.

(Nagasaki Atomic Bomb Aftermath)

On August 6th, 1945, the United States military dropped its first atomic bomb, called the Little Boy, on the city of Hiroshima, its radioactive heat instantly destroying the whole city. It stunned the world, but Japan answered with silence. The response to the silence was The Fat Man, a bigger atomic bomb that was dropped on Nagasaki three days later, on August 9th, 1945. The Soviet troops were also approaching on the other side, and on August 14th, 1945, Japan declared surrender, thus finally ending the Second World War. September 2nd, 1945, likewise, is declared as Victory in Japan Day or V-J Day.

We still wonder if it was fair to kill a million innocent people to force a country to listen. Would it not amount to a crime against humanity? Would a normal military attack not have been sufficient to defeat Japan? We are still debating over the issue. People who think it was okay argue that the Allies would have lost more than a million lives in the process of attacking Japan, and they were not ready to sacrifice so many lives. People who think the bombs should never have been dropped say it is inhuman to cause so much destruction. Do you know that surrendering is considered a very dishonorable act in the Japanese military tradition? A Japanese fighter would prefer to die rather than surrender to the enemy.

We Need a Tolerant World to Thrive and Dream

Some things, we wish we could erase from memory. But remembering them could save us from recreating those horrible times again. It, therefore, becomes our responsibility to remember the horrors of the holocaust so that we never take our freedom for granted, so that we don't assume that our loved ones will be unconditionally safe, so that we think a million times before taking democracy for granted, and so that we are vigilant about what our elected leaders are up to. It is sometimes worrying to see intolerance increasing among people in the present times. This especially happens when there is unemployment and young people get frustrated. They will then want to blame others for the misery, and we must not forget that these were similar situations that led to the Nazis' rise to power. We should be concerned that some politicians are supporting this dangerous idea across countries in the world today.

But if there is one lesson that would be the most important, it is the message of what kindness and brave action can do. While the core Nazi sympathizers were actively on a mass murder spree, unfortunately the majority of the citizens were numb, silent spectators. When something bad is happening around us, is it okay to stay silent and do nothing about it? Let us say a new kid in school is getting bullied by a group of students. Most of us are not involved and can choose to ignore it because, after all, we are not affected. Also, if we try to protect the kid, we may end up being targeted. Who would want to invite trouble anyways? What do you think our inaction is doing? Sadly, it is encouraging the crime of bullying. We are, in a way, enabling the bad deed by not doing anything about it. Unfortunately, the silence of the vast majority also led to the cruelties of the Nazis continuing. The helpless men, women, and children had no saviors.

But humanity was not getting completely

paralyzed in such bizarre times. There was a ray of hope. We had a few German citizens who took the risk of saving whoever they could. Amid the madness, some sheltered the Jews, hiding them in their houses, enabling them to reach safe places, feeding them, and showing love. This is surely the most valuable takeaway. That it is possible to be human even when the whole world seems to favor monstrosity. We wish there was more such thinking—more such courage—that shows the possibility of light at the end of a never-ending dark tunnel. We would want to know more about those people so that we can be like them.

We also learned that hatred usually starts small and soon gets into an uncontrolled spiral

of events in the most unexpected ways. When we look around us even today, we still see signs of fear and hatred, wouldn't you agree? It is a good idea to be sensitive to such behaviors and learn to identify them. Intolerance can be at individual levels where we generally don't want to be friends with particular kinds of people, or even at community levels where a certain group is labeled and not tolerated by the larger community.

The United Nations Organization

Forming a group that would be able to prevent wars was not a new idea. The League of Nations was created after the First World War with this intention. But sadly, it did not prevent the second war from breaking out. But this time we had to make it work. With nuclear weapons amongst us, the world would never recover from another such war. This time around, the United Nations Organization was headquartered in the United States, the undisputed world superpower at that time. It was established on October 24th, 1945. The main Allied powers, the United States, the United Kingdom, the Soviet Union, and China, had gotten together to create a new vision for the post-war world. Today, 193 countries out of 195 nations of the world are members. The two other nations, The Holy See and the State of Palestine, are non-member, observer states. The organization would seek to help in a balanced power order and take steps to maintain peace. Through the agreements, they promised to work towards cooperation and friendship so that everyone has a chance to develop and become a happy society. Nobody would be allowed to threaten or use force on another country in the future.

The UN as the organization is popularly

known has more main bodies to perform different functions. The General Assembly meets every year and all countries discuss the important issues in the world affecting its peace and security. The Security Council works to resolve international problems to prevent the outbreak of another war. The Economic and Social Council makes sure that every part of the world is getting a chance at developing its economy and society. We have learned that lack of opportunities gives rise to unrest, and becomes fertile ground for trouble. Just like a teacher makes sure all kids are comfortable in the class, the United Nations makes sure every country is treated fairly by others.

CHAPTER 8
BUT WHAT ABOUT ME, MY DREAMS, DON'T THEY MATTER?

• • • • • • • • •

Ordinary People When Their Country Went To War

Country A had attacked Country B; Country A's leader was not ready to negotiate with the government of Country B; Country C dropped an atomic bomb on Country D. War appears to be a straightforward event when we look at it from the outside. But amid all the sensational information, we forget that it is the lives of people like you and me that are hitting turbulence.

(launching a boat during WW2)

When the Nazi Party got absolute control over Germany, ordinary people went about their lives as usual because life at home does not change when governments change. Work, school, family, friends, entertainment, dreams, and ambitions, were all just the same, and just like ours. What makes us happy made them happy and what hurts us today hurt them just so. When the government was making decisions without asking anyone, there was nothing much people could foresee. When Hitler went about attacking neighboring countries, ordinary citizens had no particular sentiment attached. They remembered the loss of lives in the First World War, and the shortages of essential items and feared a revisit of the same scenarios.

Unlike the first war, there was no enthusiasm among ordinary people. They did not in their wildest dreams imagine what was to follow. As expected, life started getting tougher with all the rationing and the overshooting expenses to keep the war running. To keep the war going, people were forced to focus on doing things needed to have enough men for the army and sufficient ammunition, everything revolved around war and anything else was not given importance. If you were a young man, it did not matter if you wished to become a doctor, singer, or chef; you would be asked to report to fight on the frontlines.

People would get nothing but bread and potatoes—no fruits, no milk, and no sweets. Schools became irregular and eventually shut down, and the only employment choice was to participate in the war. Clothes, magazines, and toy productions stopped. Parks and playgrounds became kitchen gardens, and schools, old age homes, and concert halls became camps to abuse minority citizens. Sadly, the news was completely controlled by the government and to keep the morale high, people were misled about Jews and also lied to about the death counts of Germans in the war. Young and old people were forced to set aside dreams and their choices apart and constantly brainwashed into doing what the authorities wanted them to do.

It was not that the ordinary people agreed with their leaders, but most times they were powerless. The Nazi regime had mercy only for those who supported them. People who questioned them were murdered as well. But what is sad is that most people watched helplessly. They did not help because they did not have the courage to, and this led to more evil.

Towards the end of the war, ordinary German citizens suffered immensely. Constant bombings by Britain flattened out whole cities killing millions again, and so they would have to bear the brunt of the Soviet army advancement. Thousands of families became homeless and they would go to unknown places as refugees. Elderly people, men, women, and children, no one was spared. Germans living in other European countries began to get affected as they began to get forced out. People became victims of forced labor and life became insecure.

If this was the case in Germany, as far as the lives of the common man were concerned, the ordeal was similar whether they belonged to Japan, the Soviet Union, China, Vietnam, the United States, or any country directly or indirectly involved in the war. They were all united in suffering and sacrifice. Deeds, where people choose to be courageous, indifferent, or unfair were seen everywhere. We remember some of the good things and the bad acts of ordinary people through books and movies, but there are countless stories we will never know.

Trevor worked on a cattle farm in Australia. At thirty years old, and a father of three young kids, he loved the rough and tumble of living in the countryside. On a usual spring morning, while he unlatched the shed to let the cattle out to the meadow, the radio blared with an important-sounding message. He leaned over the hedge to hear it better. The Prime Minister announced that Great Britain had declared war on Germany and that Australia would also support Britain. Trevor did not find the news interesting since he had no idea where Germany and Britain were located and forgot about it by afternoon. But four years later he was in the trenches of Korea fighting the Japanese army. His world had twisted and turned beyond his wildest dreams. His country got involved in fighting both Germany and Japan by then. His days on the battlefield were also not what he thought they would be. There was no action and firing most of the days. In the nine months he spent on the front line, there were only a few weeks of actual defending. Every day was a boring, monotonous routine of doing rounds, repairing stuff, cleaning canteens, or playing cards with colleagues. The area where they lived was not clean, smelled of rotting garbage and unwashed clothes, and was rat infested. There would be no water for a bath, and fever and infections were common. There would be sudden changes once in a while with unpredictable attacks and colleagues being taken as prisoners of war. He did not sleep well because of the constant stress and he missed seeing his family.

How Does It Feel to Migrate and Resettle?

It's useful and at times fascinating to learn how the Second World War affected various populations in various nations. Anyone is upset when they are forced to leave their home, and it is a terrible situation because they don't know what is in store. The conflict had rather different consequences in each region, so it will be useful to have an understanding of the various experiences people had. The difficulties and positive emotions keep changing depending on the area and time.

Within the United States, the declaration of war saw a massive migration of people. Patriotic feelings were running high in every community. Everyone was keen on doing their bit to help out. Families who had settled in a particular place decided to move thousands of miles because new industries had come up to take care of war needs. Millions of young men signed up for the army and families had to replan their futures. Working conditions in the factories were not very safe. Factories that were making cars or toys would now be making ammunition or medical equipment—things would change overnight. In fact, between 1941 and 1944 there were more deaths and injuries on industrial sites than in the military. More and more women began to work in factories, which gave them opportunities to develop their skills. Children had to go through a lot of adjustments because their parents got very busy with work. Don't you think moving to a new place also gives us new opportunities? We are forced to mingle and overcome our hesitations and differences, and this opens up our minds. On the other hand, the life of the Jews and other ethnic minorities in Europe was far more traumatic and sad.

In the Diary of Anne Frank

War and suffering are uncomfortable topics for both children and adults. A diary that was discovered long after the war and the holocaust was over, belonged to a Jewish girl Anne Frank (say AN FRANK). Her writings about how she lived through those days have touched the hearts of hundreds of thousands of people since. She wrote down the happenings of her life perhaps as an outlet for dealing with the situation. Experience has taught us that writing down one's feelings has healing powers, helps us cope with difficulties, and keeps our humanness alive. We learn to process the crises around us and learn to deal with them.

This diary is important to us today because it saw the situation through the eyes of a child. Reading it showed me how sometimes the insights of children about complex matters are better than that of adults. Anne Frank, as we can imagine, surely felt a deep sense of helplessness. Questions of how and when people would get displaced or killed are frightening ones to ask oneself. Living in constant anxiety is unthinkable to many of us. We try to make sense of things using the information we already have.

She was born in Germany in 1929. Her family was forced to resettle in the Netherlands, a neighboring country, when she was very young, all because they were Jews. Her parents were liberal people and wanted the children to grow up to be knowledgeable and broad-minded. Anne and her older sister Margot grew up in a home that had a huge library. But their troubles did not end with the move. Hitler's Germany invaded the

Netherlands in 1940 and started to mistreat the Jews living there. 11-year-old Anne realized her family was again in danger. She sensed that life was about to change because they were forced to change schools, and her father was forced to close his business.

On her thirteenth birthday, June 12th, 1942, she received a nice little diary as a present. She called it Kitty and her writings began. She wrote about the restrictions being placed on the Jewish population. We discover through her writings that the family went into hiding shortly afterward as they feared for their life. They moved into the basement of her father's office building that we now know as the "Secret Annex." They had non-Jewish friends who helped them, the trouble was that it was a big risk for them as well. Hitler made it a rule that anybody found helping Jews would face the death penalty.

She wrote about her daily life, her feelings, her dreams of going back to school, her wish to be a journalist when she grew up, and the developments around her. She once mentioned how writing made her forget all her sadness and lifted her spirits. She maintained her entries for two years until her last entry on August 1st, 1944. Her family was arrested and sent to hard labor by the German police as punishment for going into hiding. From then on it was all about separation, witnessing people being sent to gas chambers, torture, starvation, disease, and death. Anne passed away in 1945 at the age of 15 in one of the concentration camps. Only her father survived the war.

The diary entries of Anne Frank have since been the subject matter of books and movies all over the world, representing the loss of childhood and the perils of war. Her voice represented the millions who suffered, no matter what their nationality or age. Imagine what the foolishness of some can do to others.

When Ordinary People Did Extraordinary Things

The brave men and women in the military have saved the lives of people, and entire villages at times, sacrificing their lives in the process or overcoming life-threatening injuries and unusual situations. It is the courage and quick thinking of brave soldiers that keep us safe and allow us to lead our lives peacefully. They sacrifice their lives so that we can have a better future. Some stories have reached us, but far more have gone untold and unknown. The world should be indebted to every soldier who put their life on the line of fire and it does not matter which side they were ordered to fight for.

The savage intentions of the Nazis were not lost to the world. Countries like Britain sensed the danger as soon as the Nazis carried out brutal killings of Jews in an event known as Kristallnacht, or Night of the Broken Glass. It happened on the night between November 8th and 9th, 1938, about a year before the war began. Jewish property was attacked and the streets were littered with broken glass. Jews were either harmed or arrested and sent to concentration camps simply because of their race. A series of unfair anti-Jew laws were enacted soon after. Unlike in today's world, news would not travel as effectively and countries found it very challenging to keep track of the internal happenings of foreign nations.

Once Britain learned of this incident they changed their immigration laws to make it easier for Jews to come to their country. Due to this unique act of the British government, over the next two years about 10,000 Jewish children were transported to Britain to remain safe until after the crisis got over. Babies and children were separated from their parents so that they would be safe. Everyone thought it would be a temporary situation and the children would be united with their families in the future. They were placed in care centers and homes of foster families. But the unimaginable happened and most of them never saw their parents again. However, this arrangement of allowing children to escape the Nazi hold stopped once Britain declared war on Germany.

Fascinatingly, these extraordinary times gave rise to heroes among very ordinary people too. They were not trained to be army men and women, but did exceptional acts. They risked their safety to make a difference in someone else's life. Bravery came from unexpected places and from out of the blue, and heroes were born out of adversities.

Nobody Knew This

One such person was Sir Nicholas Winton. He resided in London and had no reason to be on the war site to witness the horrors or keep them in his thoughts. They were far away and simple to push from one's mind. But he sensed it—he sensed the need to speak out and take action. He was 29 years old and, like most men his age, was preoccupied with organizing his upcoming ski trip. His good friend Martin Blake convinced him that he should join him in volunteering instead for an organization that was working on helping refugees from Czechoslovakia following Germany's attack. When Britain decided to let children into the country for safety, Sir Nicholas jumped at the idea. He was convinced that he could do something to try and get Czech children in as well. He felt that children should be spared from the sites of suffering, bombings, and violence. But it was easier said than done. He was told that it would be possible to allow children to be brought into Britain if he found each of them a foster home and money for their care. Over the next few months, he worked hard to convince people to help the children. It required extraordinary willpower, sacrifice, and perseverance to get to his goal, and he succeeded in getting at least 669 recorded children to safety. Many years later when the world noticed his extraordinary work, he was modest about it and believed he did not do anything remarkable. But you would agree that in reality, most people do nothing. They would stand by, watch, and look the other way!

A Story Untold—of the Japanese Americans

Like any other Japanese boy born on the soil of the United States of America, Thomas Sakamoto loved his free-spirited life in California. He was of Japanese ancestry, and his parents thought it would do him good to learn about his roots as he was growing up to be a world citizen. He would learn the culture of his ancestors and that would enrich him. He was packed and heading off to a boarding school in Japan to complete his high school years before returning to America. It all sounded like a dream plan until Japan's surprise attack in Hawaii! Before he knew it, he was drafted to an Army School in San Francisco because he knew the Japanese language. By the time he graduated, his job was waiting because the war was raging. The United States military had always known language would be a big difficulty in the event of a war. Imagine not being able to understand the secret codes and messages that an enemy was communicating while planning an attack. Their dream team would consist of people exactly like Thomas Sakamoto, citizens who would show their patriotism to America and who would thoroughly understand the moves of the Japanese, thanks to their Japanese DNA.

For Sakamoto, the next few months passed as if in a haze. He was first posted to teach Japanese to the American military officers, then sent to translate crucial information that helped in warding off Japanese attacks. Sakamoto and his colleagues served in various assignments that were held in risky conditions and dangerous locations, all the while aware that they were not being fully trusted by their other American colleagues. Their language ability was put to use to question Japanese prisoners of war, and to confuse the enemy with false commands. It was almost as if they were fighting two parallel wars—one against the land of their ancestors while proving their patriotism to their land of birth, and another against racial bias around them. There was no confusion in their minds that they owed their allegiance to America,

but they were asked to prove it time and again by people around them. Many times, the families of the Japanese Americans were interned in the camps as we learned. Their missions were top secret and most of the time their families had no clue about it. It was a tough life indeed, and their commitment and sacrifices are not spoken about when we talk of the world war; about thirty-three thousand Japanese Americans, both men and women, served in the war.

CHAPTER 9
LIFESTYLE, INVENTIONS, AND NEW IDEAS

If you think about it, life is not always straightforward. It is not possible to have good days every single day, you would agree. On some days we feel excited and joyful, some days are spent in anger or sadness, and on many days we don't feel any particular emotion strongly. In fact, we can remember the happy days because they feel different from the unhappy ones. Almost as if we would not know happiness if there was no unhappiness. It gets so bothersome when we struggle to untangle our feelings. Fights bring destruction, but strangely they also have creation buried deep inside them. It is never pleasant to be part of a war, but it is also sometimes needed to bring peace. New possibilities, dreams, and hope come after all the loss and sorrow one goes through. Change comes in positive ways too. After a nasty fight with your sibling or friend isn't there a feeling of coming out wiser from the whole thing? Whether we win or lose, we end up resolving to change certain things about the relationship that led to a fight in the first place. Now that's a good thing, isn't it?

Even though we have not seen it nor experienced it, the world war has influenced our lives. Let's try and understand how. For instance, did you realize that McDonald's was born when two brothers in America figured out how they could serve food that was easy to make and super fast to serve? Food had become expensive and there was no time to cook since everyone was working hard in factories and elsewhere to support the war. Or that the computer was developed during the war to help the army with quick and important calculations. The Nazis had the powerful Enigma machine with them which would convert top-secret messages into codes that no one else could understand. They used it to successfully launch attacks one after the other. The Allies realized that the machine's coding system had to somehow be cracked if they were to have a chance at winning. Brilliant minds worked day and night to develop machines to outwit the enemy, and we use these innovations in our computers even today.

Here We Come, the Ghost Army

"All is fair in love and war," goes the old saying. The Americans took it to heart during the war. If falsehood could save lives, history would forgive and show gratitude too. The Axis military went looking for set designers, creative artists, radio broadcasters, sound engineers, technicians, and architects who could help pull off a brilliant con job. And a top-secret mission it was! We remember these artists today for saving the lives of countless army personnel.

This Special Unit of the Allied Forces would get active on the front lines with the enemies just meters in front of them. They were masters at deception. With fake inflated tanks, jeeps, artillery, and aircraft made of rubber, using sound effects to give phony commands and sounds of rumbling machines, they stirred up enough drama to convince the enemies of the presence of a large army in close proximity. It was a play of illusions to confuse the enemy and worked wonderfully in fooling the foes for days on end. There were people to mimic army commanders to send misleading messages, ammunition designs that looked authentic, and sense deception to put the enemy off track. But we cannot hoodwink ourselves into thinking it was child's play because this unit had people with exceptionally high intelligence and talent to carry out intricate plans. Lives were sacrificed in this unit too.

They undertook a large number of such exercises in various parts of Europe to pull the wool on the Axis powers. They would place dummy artillery at places that the Germans would promptly attack. Having distracted the enemy, the Allies would then go ahead with their plans. One of  their celebrated missions was during the crossing of River Rhine where 1,100 men successfully gave the spy planes the impression of having the strength of 40,000 men!

Learning to Live in Different Ways

The modern conflict we have experienced and are now coping with is a different kind of war. It manifested as the COVID-19 pandemic.

After all, wars are not always about fighting with guns and attacks between nations. The root of the word 'war' is the Germanic verwirren which means "to perplex or confuse." And when war enters our lives, we seek solutions to the challenges that arise. When someone is compelled to do something they don't want to be doing or is forced to separate from their loved ones, it is unfair and extremely hurtful. Yet when we get desperate to find a solution to the issues troubling us, don't we think of ways of making the best of whatever is available at that time? Can you recall some creative solutions you've used to deal with a challenge?

No wonder they say necessity is the mother of invention. Difficult times made everyone look desperately for solutions and during the war, there was a huge surge in demand for inventions and new ideas. Governments made sure there was lots of money available for research. There was a super boom in the number of new medicines developed, electrical and electronic devices, and new ways of conducting business. Many modern hardware companies were formed to help the war and continue to create products that make our life easier. There was a flood of new kinds of jobs and that was very exciting. More and more people started earning well and studying, and that is a wonderful thing.

Yes, along with development came pollution, unequal earning of money, and the overcrowded cities that we see today, but then these problems are also an opportunity for us to find new solutions. Also, today we are better prepared for conflict and chaos. The United Nations Organization was formed so that countries could get together and talk out differences before jumping into war. Moreover, we now know how some of our everyday items were accidentally invented while trying to help in the war. These products looked different when they were first made because people improved them further as time went on. That is the beauty of life, though. We improve upon what already exists.

We don't think twice before pushing that plate into the microwave oven for some hot comforting meal, do we? But cooking or heating food was the last thing in mind when it was developed. It so happened that the Allies were desperate to be able to attack the enemy ships and aircraft that were bombing them. Engineers got busy trying to use electromagnetic waves to see if they can be used to knock down the enemy. Though the wave could not cause direct damage, they realized it could locate the ships and planes in the radar systems. One day an engineer in the United States named Percy Spencer was working with a magnetron tube and was intrigued that the chocolate bar in his pocket had melted when there was no heat around. He tested the tube by placing food items next to it and jumped with glee when he saw them cook. In the coming days, he developed it further to make it safe and suitable for use in restaurants and then homes, and soon the microwave oven became essential in every busy household. Today I would be helpless in a house that has no microwave!

Dr. Harry Coover was a chemical engineer working in New York. He had heard that his country was now part of the war and soon he was asked to be part of a team to help make things for the war. They were required to manufacture clear plastic for guns that would help fighters spot their targets without difficulty. They got to work but got stuck midway because the chemical was very gooey, making it cumbersome to work with. They dumped the chemical and went on to work with other materials. But the properties of that chemical group continued to fascinate Dr. Coover. In the next decade he presented the world with the 'Super Glue', the thing that could stick almost anything together. Not just that, these chemicals could be used to treat life-threatening wounds in future wars too. It could be sprayed to stop uncontrolled bleeding immediately and rejoining veins, and sealing body organs to save lives. A treasure had come out of the agony!

The Family Looks Different

Long long back, a normal household meant a big family. Grandfathers, fathers, uncles, and older brothers would go out of the house to earn a living. They could be working on farms, owning a business, working for an organization or company, or having a profession. The ladies

would mostly take care of all the household responsibilities like managing everything needed for the family, caring for children and elders, and most of the time having no time to do anything else. When the war forced people to migrate from their lands and homes, their responsibilities also changed. The big extended family started to break down and it became common to have only parents and children together in a household. Grandparents would stay back in the countryside while parents would move to cities with their children for better job possibilities. In the city, a lot of things would be different. Work for fathers and mothers increased tremendously during wartime and a lot of work became collective. They were common kitchens, food started being made in factories, child care was done by outsiders, and a lot of things got mass-produced outside the home. The living spaces began to get smaller, housework began to change and women began to learn new skills, get new education, and began going out of the houses to earn wages.

These people found ways of building temporary houses using readymade walls, roofs, and doors. This made it easier to shift and set up houses wherever they were forced to go. It was not unusual for families to change houses once every few months during disturbances. For people who could afford it, listening to the radio, and attending plays and music concerts was an option to keep them entertained. The role of women interestingly underwent a permanent change with all this turmoil. The war forced them to step out of the house to work and learn new skills, and even after the peace came back, this did not change. It meant more freedom for grandmothers, mothers, and sisters and the possibility of following their dreams. This was a happy development because women began to be treated equally to men. Migration or forced relocations, these changes see different people coming together and living side by side. Each community comes with its traditions. But when they began living in a new place, the traditions began to change. Some old practices got modified and new ones got introduced, which I guess makes the world a richer place.

Schools During Wars

When life gets difficult or dangerous, parents want to do everything it takes to keep their children safe. Not just physically safe but to have them grow up capable of taking care of themselves. The importance of educating children also grew tremendously during those times because that was the only hope for a promising tomorrow. The families in concentration camps, the ones who had migrated, and the refugees, irrespective of the part of the world they were in, all had one common aspiration - a better future for their children. It was a struggle because there wouldn't be proper buildings that could be used as schools, there were too many children with too few teachers, and stationary and facilities were always in short supply. Lessons had to be handwritten since printed books were not available, and they had to figure out what to teach. Often the information was aimed at brainwashing students to think in a certain way.

In the Japanese internment camps in the United States, the culture of respecting education and teachers was held high. Children were expected to be sincere in their work and would go to school in clean clothes despite all the difficulties. In Great Britain, many children were shifted from cities to villages to be kept safe from bombings and air raids. They would move from place to place depending on whether the attacks would happen sooner or later schooling got disrupted multiple times. Often school buildings would be used by the army for shelter or imprisoning enemies. Parents would collect children in their house basements and appoint teachers to teach them. There were times when classes would be conducted with everyone wearing gas masks. During free time they would

have to sacrifice play to collect donations, make kitchen gardens, or knit gloves, and socks to be sent to the army. When children got into their late teens, there was a very high chance that they would be asked to stop studying and join the army, voluntary organizations, or even work in farms and industries.

Overcoming Despair Through Sports

Reading about wars sometimes made me grumpy but one day I was pleasantly surprised to read a report on how people experiencing wars used sports as a way of finding happiness. For the common people as well as soldiers on the battlefield, the common thing was that life was not in their control and had become dangerous. The training sessions of soldiers were intense and the possibilities of accidents were high. During such times, distracting the mind and moving the body for playing a sport was a very effective method of managing themselves. I believe it is because playing helps me find peace of mind when I am going through tough days. Being part of team sports helped groups in the communities and army camps everywhere to help them forget the depressing realities and overcome their sense of despair. Baseball became a religion for the Japanese internees and was an effective way of overcoming the trauma of unfair treatment. People of all ages took part in sports and this became a source of comfort. Many talented sportsmen had to enlist in the war and sacrifice their sports, it is sad that they could not do what they loved, and their dreams got nipped in the bud. But many of them used their ability to play to guide their friends in coping on the front lines, after all, sports teach us to hope and build life skills.

During those trying times, many more people discovered their skills, and athletics is still promoted as a valuable life skill today for good reason. Many kids still found a way to play during active wartime and across continents. Playing among the debris was really fascinating for them. They would create their tiny games and toys out of leftover materials since war always meant a shortage of money. They would play hopscotch, marbles, and jump rope in the empty spaces, and cards, monopoly, and scrabbles for hours at a stretch when they were forced to stay indoors. Playing helps to heal, and we are not talking about addictive online games here. Since there is something about moving your body that helps the mind every youngster needs the magic recipe, which involves getting out into the field, and learning how to interact with real people.

CHAPTER 10
FIVE NATIONS, FIVE LIVES

• • • • • • • • • •

Yumi's Brother, Japan 1942

Yumi was a nine-year-old girl. The year was 1942. She lived in a tiny little village near the mountains. Like most people in the village, her parents were farmers and not very rich. She had three pairs of dresses and they were all hand-me-downs of her elder sister. That winter she could sense the tension growing around her because all the hushed conversations in the village were about Japan attacking America. Some people were feeling proud, some were very worried but nobody dared to speak their minds. Yumi's twenty-three-year-old brother had been asked to report for military duty. It was heartbreaking to see him go, but there was no choice. Yumi could not bear to think of not seeing her brother every day, she was so used to following his footsteps everywhere, collecting mushrooms while he cheerfully dug at the hard soil in the winter mornings, and chasing birds together while helping father harvest rice from the lush green fields.

(Mount Fuji, Japan)

She loved her country but did not understand why things had to be so hard on them. There were strict rules everywhere; her older school friends had to go to factories after school to help in making army uniforms, playtime got canceled, summer holidays became work time, and food became more and more difficult to get. Yumi would be sent along with friends to collect old clothes and paper from neighbors so that they could be sent for recycling. Mother could no longer afford to get medicines for her headaches and father had to work double hours on the farm now that his son was away. She wondered why rice had to be submitted to the association, even when they did not have enough for themselves. Yumi woke up every morning and sat on the doorstep of their tiny house, hoping to see her brother walk back home through the dusty road that led to the front yard. A year passed, and she still had not given up hope. One late evening, someone came to see her father. He was to travel to a faraway town to bring his son's ashes back. Yumi's brother had died in the war.

Claus's Friend Goes Missing, Germany 1940

Berlin, Germany. The year was 1940, and Amos would be turning twelve in the winter. He always remembered his extended family as one big jolly gang, but of late something was amiss. The smiles looked strained and the family gatherings were getting more somber. Amos did not feel like getting excited about his upcoming birthday, he knew there would be no celebrations. There would be so many worried discussions going on in his family. "They seem to simply hate Jews. They don't want us here and I am worried about the children," he heard his father tell his uncle one day. Mother would not let the kids go to the market alone anymore. Every other day his family would hear news about their relatives being forced to shut their businesses or getting thrown out of their own houses. Amos would wake up in the middle of the night with terrible dreams.

(Oberbaum Bridge, Berlin)

Claus lived two streets away and was Amos's best friend in school since the time they were four years old. Their football dreams got them together after school hours; all they could think of were ways of making it to the inter-school team in their high school years. News of the war was in the air, and for the first time in their lives and much to their discomfort, Amos and Claus began identifying themselves as Jew and Aryan, all because everybody suddenly started to think in terms of the race they belonged to. The radio, family get-togethers, casual talk between friends, everything seemed to veer around the same thing: fear and suspicion. It didn't make any sense to them, and it felt so wrong, but the new reality could not be brushed away. The games and the meetings between the two slowly began to get shaky, with no logic to it, but clouded with a strange sense of fear; it was as if an invisible epidemic of hate had taken over ordinary people. The school had abruptly been declared shut and Claus did not hear from Amos for three full weeks. One sleepy afternoon, agitation got the better of him and he snuck out to run across to the street where Amos lived. As he approached the ever-so-familiar blue house, he realized the furniture of the house was scattered around on the front porch for auction by the authorities. The family had fled overnight due to threats on their lives, no one knew where to. Claus was left to live with the hurt of losing his dear friend.

Haunting Memories to Live With, Vietnam 1943

One tiny country in Southeast Asia that got tragically entangled in a complicated situation in the Second World War was Vietnam. It had already been colonized by France for many years. As you would guess by now Japan had set its eyes on making the country its own. Trang was a chirpy little girl with silky hair and a melodious voice. She walked around with gold-rimmed glasses, unusual for a ten-year-old. "Trang, are you there in the class?" her new French teacher called out her name from the register. "I am sorry miss.. it is pronounced

Chang," she meekly corrected her, like she had to with every foreigner who got her name wrong. Why me? she would mutter to herself every time, weary of this uninvited ordeal.

The year was 1940, and emotions ran high all around her. Japan's invasion had divided the people of her country. Her father vociferously wanted his country free of French colonial rule and spent his days passionately convincing his friends to volunteer in the struggle. Initially, he spent most of his time outside the home, and then eventually began staying away altogether. Trang did not like it one bit when people said he was risking his life. Mother would not tell her much but would be worried all the time. She learned from her friends that a lot of people like her father lived in remote jungles and made dangerous plans to fight the government. The problems did not end here. Her uncle, her father's younger brother, was very angry that her father was against the French. She was confused because although she gathered that the armies of three different countries, France,

Japan, and the United States, were all in Vietnam, she could not figure out why. As if the war outside was not enough, there were fights within the family also with everyone taking different sides. Trang did not get to see her little cousin for the next fifteen years and she was all grown up by the time her father returned home. But he was never the same. He had been tortured and had injuries all over his body. His gaze looked almost alien, he screamed in his sleep, and he could not concentrate on anything anymore.This continued until his death many years later. Trang had got back her father and lost him at the same time.

The Day it Rained Parachutes, Netherlands 1944

Something fancy is always welcome even when we are boggled with chaos. Egon and his sister Dael were out on their tiny farm digging for potatoes. It was no fun doing their lessons every day when school was shut down for so long and Mamma surely would do with some help. The enthusiastic chore was intruded on by an unlikely play of shadows in the autumn morning. Dael looked up expecting to see clouds dance by. She got up and stood motionless. Egon sensed the tension in her breath and looked up to where her eyes had locked themselves. "Are they geese, Egonee?" Dael finally managed to ask. Before Egon could gather his wits to guess, they saw the figures getting larger. "Run, Dael, run!" said Egon as he caught hold of his sister's hands and ran towards their house. That day the villages of Arnhem were in for the most spectacular sights they had seen in their life. Thousands of paratroopers descended from the skies as if from heaven to liberate their lands from the Nazi clutch, except that things didn't quite go to plan. Dael and Egon could see the elders in the family showing excitement at the news of the soldiers landing. Over the next four days, the children were not allowed to step out of the house and they heard the news of dangerous fighting in the streets. They could overhear elders talking of brave soldiers dying and being buried in the village.

Operation Market Garden was an elaborate plan drawn by the Allies to surprise the German troops with a massive airborne attack. They calculated that if they get about 50,000 personnel to land into the enemy terrain from the skies, it would help the ground army to capture the important bridges and huge areas on the south side of the Netherlands. By the way, did you know that Holland is an informal name of The Netherlands, almost like a nickname?

Everything appeared to be in place. A simultaneous attack from the sky and land would surely unsettle the Germans. Unfortunately, the surprise backfired because the German army seemed to be in good shape and resisting well. They successfully blocked the paratroopers from moving toward their targets. To add to the agony, the cloudy weather did not allow timely landing, and the radios of the men went blank making communication difficult and giving the enemies time to plan a counterattack. Though the Allies were successful in breaking into German territory, the operation resulted in a lot of loss of lives and therefore not a happy memory.

Sea, an Escape? Denmark 1943

When everyone appears to be acting strangely, not everything is doom and gloom. Numerous tales encourage us to return to believing in hope. Stories of Germans hiding Jewish families in their houses during the Holocaust, giving medical treatment to wounded enemy soldiers because humanity comes first, and taking risks to save lives, are examples of the good deeds of the common people. Alma lived with her parents and two brothers in Denmark. They belonged to the people of the Roma community, which were also called gypsies. The Nazis targeted them as an inferior race, just like they did the Jews. The year was 1943 and by now people knew all about what the Nazis were up to. Even the Germans were fed up and some of them would leak important information to try and save people as much as they could. Alma's family was woken up in the middle of the night by their neighbors. "Take your belongings and come with me. Don't ask questions, you are going to Sweden!" Alma would never forget the horse voice of urgency in the man's voice. He thrust some papers into her father's hands. All she remembers is her father asking them to run as fast as they could while he hurriedly took some warm clothes and all the cash he could lay his hands on from the cupboard. They spent the rest of the night walking to a village near the seashore. Before sunrise, they were onboard a ferry with about 25-odd families like them.

They were lucky to have been sent away from Denmark before the German army got to them. The people of Denmark showed remarkable presence of mind and willpower to save their minority citizens. It was regular people like you and me who got together and made arrangements to take them to the safe land. They rushed to hide their neighbors in safe places and then ferry them in small boats through the sea to Sweden. Nobody would be able to harm them there. After several weeks, around 8,000 families were sent to safety by the so-called ordinary people. George Ferdinand Duckwitz, a German diplomat was the man who had secretly informed the Danes of the Nazi plan.

CONCLUSION

· · · · · • · • · • · · ·

Sometimes it is tempting to not look into the past. We think that people were different back then and we would behave in another way today. But then it helps a lot when we know to recognize patterns. For instance, it is helpful to know that Adolf Hitler did not exactly plan to kill millions of people. His ideas started a chain reaction: he found the support of some people, and got one thing to lead to another, all ending in massive destruction. If only someone could foresee and stop the idea in its initial stage! When things happen in the world that confuse and frighten us, we need to remember the past so that we can make informed choices. And so it becomes all the more important that we keep these memories alive. Yes, they hurt, but remembering that is an important way to prevent future regrets, and so preserving the past paves the way for a better tomorrow.

(WW2 planes)

What, therefore, have we learned from the war? That people get into fights for many reasons. Sometimes it could be to protect themselves. You would not sit back and watch if someone snatched your bag on a lonely street, you would try and get even. You need to get back what belongs to you, but then you need to decide how it is to be done. Whether you take the law into your own hands or get the police to do their job is a matter of choice. In any case, we need to act fairly and look at the best possible trade-off.

I agree that society may sometimes have baffling challenges. Let us think about some potential solutions. They would include, among other things, the fact that a democratic system is the safest way to manage society and our issues. But what exactly does democracy mean? It is about ensuring that everyone has a voice and is actively listening. It is a healthy democracy when an individual or group can't settle on anything without asking others for their opinions. It is a situation where I cannot dominate just because I can. It is all about ordinary people having the power to decide the kind of government they want. This makes the people in power always answerable to the citizens because otherwise they will get elected out. But this also means that people have to be watchful. They should voice their opinion, ask uncomfortable questions, and always be ready for a healthy debate. Because if people are not vigilant, the leaders will become more and more controlling and get more power in their hands. If a country has a weak leader who cannot keep democracy strong, then it is time for all of us to be careful.

But maintaining democracy is difficult and can look messy at times. Decisions are not made quickly because there is much talking and debating. We can lose patience with all the indecision. When Germany invaded Poland at the beginning of the war, it took democratic Britain and France eight long months to launch action against Germany. The lesson we learn here is that late action can be of little use. But a wrong quick decision has worse consequences, as we have seen in dictatorships. Democracies have to be in good health to be effective, and for that, everyone has to actively participate in the process. The world continues to have problems. Hurting others is sadly not a thing that ended with the last world war. What happened does not seem enough to get us to remember the pain of conflict. People are continuing to get thrown out of their land in the name of religion and race, the freedom of the people and the press continues to get stifled, and democracy gets threatened now and then. We still see military and terrorist attacks here and there. But we should not forget that we all have a choice to create change for the better.

Reading or watching documentaries and movies about tumultuous events like the war in general, and the holocaust in particular, does give us a feel of what happened, but sometimes it makes the war look like just another story. An actual visit to a World War Memorial affects you at a different level. If you could manage to do so sometime in the future, you must give yourself that chance. It brings us closer to the real experience of what people went through, it makes it a very personal journey. It makes one almost feel anguish and can shake us to the core. We get to see pictures of people when they were suffering the war, the samples of personal things they used, like clothes, belongings, and weapons. We get to see the letters they wrote to their families and their grief of separation. And no matter which side of the war they were on, agony and pain was common. It makes me question the purpose of war when I see this. Weirdly, it is so easy to hate others when we are told things about them, but when we bother to get to know them better, our thinking changes completely.

Unfortunately, the ordeal does not end when the war is over. People continue to suffer long after and the memories continue to have an effect on whatever they do. Doctors and researchers have shown how the social conditions and mental health of people who experience war are affected and pieces of the war stay with them forever. Some of the traumas carry on into future generations also. Children grow up in families that have members struggling to cope, and it affects them, too. Do we want things like this to repeat? Surely, we can

use our imagination to solve problems in a better way.

Bystander or Upstander: What Do You Say?

Bad behavior does not belong to wartime alone. We see it every day and everywhere. Within ourselves, in our houses, outside, by known and unknown people. Sometimes unfair behavior is so subtle that it is difficult to pinpoint and call it out. But how do we learn to recognize bad behavior? It's a feeling that comes up within us when we see it, right?

When minorities were being given a bad deal through subtle restrictions, spreading rumors, and discrimination in Nazi Germany, people could feel it, but they did nothing. By doing nothing, they ended up encouraging it and finally letting horrible things happen. Do we want to continue to be that way as human beings? Do we let things happen by doing nothing about it? After all, Adolf Hitler, the symbol of cruelty, was one human being just like you and me; his supporters were ordinary people like us. Then where did the monstrosity come from? It sadly came from the inaction of ordinary people. People like you and me looked the other way when humanity was being violated.

When we see poverty around us or in countries of Africa we know that it is not natural. We understand that opportunities have been denied to them because powerful nations and people have an advantage over them. We find unfairness when we bother to look deeper into the issues. But then we choose to look away because it does not concern us. The truth is that each of us, the so-called ordinary people, has the power to make a difference; it is just that we are made to believe that we do not. We can raise our voices or take a stand against discrimination through our writing, singing, and choosing not to buy products from companies that discriminate or use unethical means to profit. We can choose not to fall for marketing gimmicks, propaganda, and popular trends that hurt voiceless communities.

We have good and bad things to remember about the war. Inventions were great, racism was suppressed, and dictatorships ended but there was such a lot of destruction that brought it to our wit's end. It, however, has taught us to handle crises better and that is a very useful thing. Disasters like the pandemic, earthquakes, floods, and such natural calamities have to be handled with good strategy. The army has built that resilience thanks to experiences of war. If only we could learn our lessons without such mistakes. Mankind had paid a heavy price. The winners and losers had equally suffered. It was mind-boggling, everyone was weary of war and clearly in the mood for a new dawn. Apart from the fact that more than 80 million people from both sides of the war lost their lives, the war changed the lives of almost every living person in every single country, and would also continue to shape the future for a long time. The weapons have become extremely powerful now and so the price we pay in case there is another war will be unimaginably huge. Today we have technology capable of destroying whole cities in a matter of minutes. In a world that has enough for everyone's needs but not enough for everyone's greed, peace, conversation, and love are the only weapons we have at our disposal. Let us use them to make the world a better place.

ABOUT THE AUTHOR

Storytellers with their deft fingers on the pulse of history and mythology make up the impassioned collective known as **History Brought Alive**. Facts are presented precisely with the intellect of a historian, but never at the expense of the audience's emotions. The narrator shares the dilemmas, anxieties, hopes, and joys of the impressionable reader, much like a devoted grandma who understands the innermost thoughts of the youngster listening to her. Every historical turning point is described in a very personal way so that children develop sensitivity to human emotions and appreciation of circumstances along with building their language skills. They will get a sense of history and culture and this will reflect on their personality and positively impact their life choices. Believe us when we say compassionate storytelling is contagious. It rubs off on the reader as well!

REFERENCES

6 Inventions Made for War That Are Now Used By Civilians. (2022, July 18). VeteranLife | Welcome Home. https://veteranlife.com/military-history/inventions-made-for-war/

Adamson, D. (n.d.). The Holocaust: remembering the powerful acts of "ordinary people." The Conversation. Retrieved April 30, 2023, from https://theconversation.com/the-holocaust-remembering-the-powerful-acts-of-ordinary-people-196076

Asia for Educators. (2009). Japan's Quest for Power and World War II in Asia | Asia for Educators | Columbia University. Columbia.edu. http://afe.easia.columbia.edu/special/japan_1900_power.htm

Berenbaum, M. (2018, January 25). Why Must We Remember the Holocaust? Because Democracy is Precious. Facingtoday.facinghistory.org. https://facingtoday.facinghistory.org/why-must-we-remember-the-holocaust-because-democracy-is-precious

CWGC. (n.d.). Stories from Operation Market Garden & the Battle for Arnhem. CWGC. https://www.cwgc.org/our-work/blog/stories-from-operation-market-garden-the-battle-for-arnhem/

Dittmann, M. (2004, October). What makes good people do bad things? Https://Www.apa.org. https://www.apa.org/monitor/oct04/goodbad

Education and Sports | DPLA. (2015). Dp.la. https://dp.la/exhibitions/japanese-internment/education-sports/sports

Hampson, R. (2015, July 18). 70 years later: How World War II changed America. USA TODAY; USATODAY. https://www.usatoday.com/story/news/nation/2015/07/18/70-years-later-how-world-war-ii-changed-america/30334203/

Harry Coover | Lemelson-MIT Program. (2011). Mit.edu. https://lemelson.mit.edu/resources/harry-coover

Hevesiová, S. (n.d.). Writing Down the War: The Child's Perspective. Retrieved November 7, 2022, from https://dergipark.org.tr/tr/download/article-file/45388

Hicks, S. (2003, March 20). Simon Partner: The WW II Home Front In Japan. Duke.edu. https://today.duke.edu/2003/03/japan_lecture0321.html

History.com Editors. (2018, August 21). Benito Mussolini. HISTORY.com; A&E Television Networks. https://www.history.com/topics/world-war-ii/benito-mussolini

Holocaust Memorial Day Trust | Sir Nicholas Winton. (n.d.). https://www.hmd.org.uk/resource/sir-nicholas-winton/

Holocaust Memorial Day Trust | The Kindertransport and refugees. (2019). Hmd.org.uk. https://www.hmd.org.uk/learn-about-the-holocaust-and-genocides/the-holocaust/kindertransport-refugees/

Home and Family | DPLA. (2015). Dp.la. https://dp.la/exhibitions/japanese-internment/home-family

Imperial War Museums. (2018). Growing Up In The Second World War. Imperial War Museums. https://www.iwm.org.uk/history/growing-up-in-the-second-world-war

Invasion of France – The Holocaust Explained: Designed for schools. (n.d.). https://www.theholocaustexplained.org/life-in-nazi-occupied-europe/the-second-world-war/invasion-of-france/

Khan Academy . (2017). The United Nations. Khan Academy. https://www.khanacademy.org/humanities/us-history/rise-to-world-power/us-wwii/a/the-united-nations

Klein, C. (2022, March 3). The Top-Secret WWII Unit That Fooled the Nazis. HISTORY. https://www.history.com/news/ghost-army-world-war-ii

Kuster, A. M. (2021, May 19). Text - H.R.707 - 117th Congress (2021-2022): Ghost Army Congressional Gold Medal Act. Www.congress.gov. https://www.congress.gov/bill/117th-congress/house-bill/707/text

Lee, T. B. (2014, September 1). 75 years ago, Hitler invaded Poland. Here's how it happened. Vox; Vox. https://www.vox.com/2014/9/1/6084029/hitlers-invasion-of-poland-explained

Life in Germany during World War Two - CCEA - GCSE History Revision - CCEA. (n.d.). BBC Bitesize. https://www.bbc.co.uk/bitesize/guides/zp47pbk/revision/1

National geographic. (2016, August 8). Attack on Pearl Harbor. History. https://kids.nationalgeographic.com/history/article/pearl-harbor

Ordinary Heroes. (n.d.). ShadowLight. Retrieved April 30, 2023, from https://www.myshadowlight.org/ordinary-heroes

Religious Practices. (n.d.). Digital Public Library of America. https://dp.la/exhibitions/japanese-internment/religious-practices/tradition

Smilde, K. (2020, May 20). What is the holocaust? Anne Frank Website; Anne Frank House. https://www.annefrank.org/en/anne-frank/go-in-depth/what-is-the-holocaust/

State of Oregon: World War II - Rationing: A Necessary But Hated Sacrifice. (n.d.). Sos.oregon.gov. https://sos.oregon.gov/archives/exhibits/ww2/Pages/services-rationing.aspx

The Accidental Invention of the Microwave | commercial microwave. (2017, December 29). Celcook. https://celcook.ca/the-accidental-invention-of-the-microwave/

The National WWII Museum. (2017, June 22). The Path to Pearl Harbor. The National WWII Museum | New Orleans. https://www.nationalww2museum.org/war/articles/path-pearl-harbor

The National WWII Museum. (2018). Rationing | The National WWII Museum | New Orleans. The National WWII Museum | New Orleans. https://www.nationalww2museum.org/war/articles/rationing

The start of the Second World War: Germany invades Poland | Anne Frank House. (n.d.). Www.annefrank.org. https://www.annefrank.org/en/timeline/24/the-start-of-the-second-world-war-germany-invades-poland/

The Untold Story of the Japanese Americans Who Fought in World War II. (2022, September 2). Time. https://time.com/6209972/japanese-americans-fought-world-war-ii-history/

The WWII Home Front (U.S. National Park Service). (2017). Nps.gov. https://www.nps.gov/articles/the-wwii-home-front

United States Holocaust Memorial Museum. (2018). How did Public Opinion About Entering World War II Change Between 1939 and 1941? - Americans - United States Holocaust Memorial Museum. Ushmm.org. https://exhibitions.ushmm.org/americans-and-the-holocaust/us-public-opinion-world-war-II-1939-1941

United States Holocaust Memorial Museum. (2019a). Kindertransport, 1938–1940. Ushmm.org. https://encyclopedia.ushmm.org/content/en/article/kindertransport-1938-40

United States Holocaust Memorial Museum. (2019b). Rescue in Denmark. Ushmm.org. https://encyclopedia.ushmm.org/content/en/article/rescue-in-denmark

VIEW OF WAR DIFFERENT FROM CHILD'S PERSPECTIVE – Daily Press. (n.d.). Www.dailypress.com. Retrieved April 30, 2023, from

https://www.dailypress.com/news/dp-xpm-19910121-1991-01-21-9101220177-story.html

warfare | Etymology, origin and meaning of warfare by etymonline. (n.d.). Www.etymonline.com. Retrieved April 30, 2023, from https://www.etymonline.com/word/warfare

Wikipedia Contributors. (2018, October 8). Nazi concentration camps. Wikipedia; Wikimedia Foundation. https://en.wikipedia.org/wiki/Nazi_concentration_camps

World War I. (2018, December 18). Wikipedia; Wikimedia Foundation. https://en.wikipedia.org/wiki/World_War_I

FREE BONUS FROM HBA: EBOOK BUNDLE

Greetings!

First, thank you for reading our books.

Now, we invite you to join our VIP list. As a welcome gift we offer the History & Mythology eBook Bundle below for free. Plus, you can be the first to receive new books and exclusives! Remember it's 100% free to join.

Simply click the link below to join.

https://www.subscribepage.com/hba

Keep up to date with us on:
YouTube: History Brought Alive
Facebook: History Brought Alive
www.historybroughtalive.com

OTHER BOOKS BY HISTORY BROUGHT ALIVE

Available now in Ebook, Paperback, Hardcover, and Audiobook in all regions.

For Kids:

Other books:

WORLD WAR 2 HISTORY FOR KIDS

We sincerely hope you enjoyed our new book ***"World War 2 History Brought Alive"***. We would greatly appreciate your feedback with an honest review at the place of purchase.

First and foremost, we are always looking to grow and improve as a team. It is reassuring to hear what works, as well as receive constructive feedback on what should improve. Second, starting out as an unknown author is exceedingly difficult, and Amazon reviews go a long way toward making the journey out of anonymity possible. Please take a few minutes to write an honest review.

Best regards,

History Brought Alive

http://historybroughtalive.com/

www.ingramcontent.com/pod-product-compliance
Lightning Source LLC
Chambersburg PA
CBHW050341010526
44119CB00049B/640